Milady's Standard Esthetics: Advanced Exam Review

Milady

Australia • Brazil • Japan • Korea • Mexico • Singapore • Spain • United Kingdom • United States

Milady's Standard Esthetics: Advanced Exam Review, 1E

Author(s): Milady

President, Milady: Dawn Gerrain

Publisher: Erin O'Connor

Acquisitions Editor: Martine Edwards

Product Manager: Jessica Burns

Editorial Assistant: Elizabeth Edwards

Director of Beauty Industry Relations: Sandra Bruce

Senior Marketing Manager: Gerard McAvey

Marketing Specialist: Erica Conley

Marketing Coordinator: Matthew McGuire

Production Director: Wendy Troeger

Senior Content Project Manager: Nina Tucciarelli

Art Director: Joy Kocsis

For product information and technology assistance, contact us at **Professional & Career Group Customer Support, 1-800-648-7450**

For permission to use material from this text or product, submit all requests online at **cengage.com/permissions.**
Further permissions questions can be e-mailed to **permissionrequest@cengage.com.**

Exam View® and Exam View Pro® are registered trademarks of FSCreations, Inc. Windows is a registered trademark of the Microsoft Corporation used herein under license. Macintosh and Power Macintosh are registered trademarks of Apple Computer, Inc. Used herein under license.

Library of Congress Control Number: 2007941007

ISBN-13: 978-1-4283-1978-3
ISBN-10: 1-4283-1978-6

Delmar
5 Maxwell Drive
Clifton Park, NY 12065-2919
USA

Cengage Learning products are represented in Canada by Nelson Education, Ltd.

For your lifelong learning solutions, visit
milady.cengage.com

Visit our corporate website at **milady.cengage.com.**

Notice to the Reader

Printed in Canada
1 2 3 4 5 WC 11 10 09

Milady's Standard Esthetics: Advanced Exam Review

Foreword

Milady's Standard Esthetics: Advanced Exam Review follows the type of skin care questions most frequently used by states and by the national testing, conducted under the auspices of the National-Interstate Council of State Boards of Cosmetology.

This review book is designed to be of major assistance to students in preparing for the state license examinations and future career path. The exclusive concentration on multiple-choice test items reflects the fact that all state board examinations and national testing examinations are confined to this type of question.

Questions on the state board examinations in different states will not be exactly like these and may not touch upon all the information covered in this review. But students who diligently study and practice their work as taught in the classroom and who use this book for test preparation and review should receive higher grades on both classroom and license examinations.

The answers to the questions are found at the end of the book.

Part 1: Orientation

CHAPTER 1—CHANGES IN ESTHETIC OPPORTUNITIES

1. Which of the following statements about advanced esthetics is true?
   a. estheticians are losing their professional footing to doctors
   b. poorly educated estheticians can learn from the public
   c. baby boomers have increased the demand for modern esthetics
   d. all answers   ____

2. Which of the following words means to scatter, sprinkle, or moisten?
   a. spagere   c. sanitas
   b. espa   d. all answers   ____

3. Which of the following statements about early spas is NOT true?
   a. spa treatments began with bathhouses in ancient Greece
   b. balnea bathhouses in Rome were used at home
   c. Roman bathing culture originally had a medicinal focus
   d. most bathhouses were protected when the Roman Empire fell   ____

4. During the 16th century, public baths declined in popularity for all of the following reasons EXCEPT:
   a. wealthy citizens preferred natural mineral springs
   b. water was lacking due to an international drought
   c. bathhouses were thought to cause diseases
   d. firewood to heat the bathhouses was scarce   ____

5. The treatments developed by Father Sebastian Kneipp were based on the belief that:
   a. excess blood restores balance and good health
   b. bathhouses caused such diseases as syphilis
   c. water could eliminate body waste and cure disease
   d. drinking large amounts of water had curative effects   ____

6. Which of the following professionals is responsible for choosing and stocking the appropriate numbers and kinds of cosmetic products for a spa or salon?
   a. cosmetic buyer   c. makeup artist
   b. sales representative   d. esthetics instructor   ____

7. All of the following are job duties of the state licensing inspector EXCEPT:
   a. investigate complaints   c. enforce regulations
   b. prepare examinations   d. demonstrate products   ____

8. For which of the following positions are organizational skills most critical?
   a. permanent makeup artist
   b. manager or salesperson
   c. store sales representative
   d. beauty magazine columnist
   _____

9. A professional who partners with a dermatologist or plastic surgeon to devise skin-care routines and apply corrective makeup is a(n):
   a. permanent makeup artist
   b. esthetician
   c. medical esthetician
   d. spa owner
   _____

10. Questions like, "Where did this information come from?" and "Is this information based on opinion or fact?" support which step of the critical thinking process?
    a. examine the evidence
    b. clarify the problem
    c. execute the solution
    d. gather the facts
    _____

11. In order, the first three steps of the critical thinking process are:
    a. fact gathering, problem clarification, outcome definition
    b. problem clarification, fact gathering, evidence examination
    c. evidence examination, fact gathering, problem clarification
    d. problem clarification, outcome definition, evidence examination
    _____

12. At what point in the critical thinking process does the esthetician identify what the client wants and needs?
    a. gather the facts
    b. examine the evidence
    c. define solutions
    d. clarify the problem
    _____

13. In the acronym SOAP, the S stands for:
    a. solution
    b. simplicity
    c. subjective
    d. solitude
    _____

14. In which step of the SOAP method of documenting critical thinking do estheticians capture what they observe?
    a. procedure
    b. objective
    c. subjective
    d. assessment
    _____

15. In the field of esthetics, "soft" skills are based on:
    a. intuition
    b. education
    c. training
    d. all answers
    _____

16. A client who wants to feel calm, soothed, and relaxed after an esthetics treatment wants treatment that is:
    a. disease focused
    b. segmented
    c. age oriented
    d. holistic

    _____

17. A holistic provider does all of the following EXCEPT:
    a. focuses on personal comfort during treatment
    b. smiles and maintains eye contact
    c. uses clients' names in conversation
    d. models a calm, nurturing, and confident demeanor

    _____

18. Estheticians who wish to treat themselves holistically should do all of the following EXCEPT:
    a. visualize a state of happiness
    b. converse more during treatments
    c. write a mission statement
    d. stand up straight and laugh

    _____

19. Under the Health Insurance Portability and Accountability Act (HIPAA) of 1996, which of the following is NOT true?
    a. all states must comply with all portions of the legislation
    b. providers must describe how they will use personal medical information
    c. providers determine which medical records are released to patients
    d. all employees must take HIPAA training through their employers

    _____

20. All of the following are federal sources of esthetics information EXCEPT:
    a. Occupational Safety and Health Administration
    b. National Accrediting Commission of Cosmetology Arts and Sciences
    c. National-Interstate Council of State Boards of Cosmetology
    d. International Therapy Examination Council

    _____

Part 2: General Sciences

CHAPTER 2—INFECTION CONTROL

1. Which of the following pieces of legislation was originally called the "Safety Bill of Rights"?
   a. Occupational Safety and Health Act
   b. Chemical Right-to-Know Law
   c. Bloodborne Pathogens Standard
   d. none of these ____

2. All of the following are key elements of IRS Form SS-8 EXCEPT:
   a. behavioral control
   b. employee proficiency
   c. worker/firm relationship
   d. financial control ____

3. Which of the following key elements of the Bloodborne Pathogens Standard requires employers to provide employees protective devices?
   a. follow-up after exposure
   b. Standard Precautions
   c. work practice controls
   d. cleanliness of work areas ____

4. According to the Bloodborne Pathogens Standard, which of the following statements about the hepatitis B vaccine is NOT true?
   a. estheticians are in the Group One Classification
   b. estheticians working outside the medical office have no hepatitis B risk
   c. employees must be given the vaccine within ten days of starting work
   d. hepatitis B vaccine is given in three doses over a six-month period ____

5. According to the Bloodborne Pathogens Standard, all of the following are considered personal protective equipment EXCEPT:
   a. splash guards
   b. goggles
   c. gloves
   d. lab coats ____

6. When exposure to a potentially infectious substance has occurred, OSHA requires all of the following EXCEPT:
   a. testing of the employee for HBV, HCV, and HIV
   b. offering of prophylaxis or HB vaccine to the employee
   c. counseling of the employee on transmission precautions
   d. recording of the source's activities for 30 years ____

7. Which of the following statements about hepatitis is NOT true?
   a. hepatitis infection is more likely than HIV infection
   b. many hepatitis strains have no symptoms
   c. hepatitis is caused by a bacterial infection
   d. viruses causing hepatitis include A, B, C, and H   _____

8. The least dangerous form of hepatitis that is always acute is hepatitis:
   a. C   c. E
   b. A   d. B   _____

9. Which hepatitis virus is the major cause of all hepatitis cases arising from transfusions and intravenous drug use?
   a. C   c. B
   b. E   d. G   _____

10. The form of hepatitis that is treated with bed rest and avoidance of intimate contact is hepatitis:
   a. D   c. A
   b. C   d. B   _____

11. Which of the following statements about HIV is NOT true?
   a. a person with HIV may exhibit no symptoms for months
   b. HIV is spread through unprotected sex and needle sharing
   c. HIV destroys the body's ability to fight infections
   d. the main sources of HIV infection are semen and saliva   _____

12. Which of the following statements about tuberculosis is NOT true?
   a. bovine tuberculosis is carried by unpasteurized milk
   b. tuberculosis is part of the hepatitis family
   c. over one-third of the world has the tuberculosis bacterium
   d. tuberculosis is a very resistive virus   _____

13. Which of the following statements about resident microorganisms is true?
   a. they can become opportunistic
   b. they are known as "abnormal flora"
   c. most are found in the deep epidermal layers
   d. scrubbing will completely remove them   _____

14. Which of the following statements about transient microorganisms is true?
   a. they are removed through hand washing
   b. waxing can increase susceptibility to them
   c. they are easily picked up on hands and clothing
   d. all answers   _____

15. Resident and transient microorganisms differ in that:
    a. resident microorganisms can become opportunistic
    b. resident microorganisms are removed through hand washing
    c. transient microorganisms cannot be pathogenic
    d. all answers   _____

16. When an organism enters the body through a fresh wound or
    nonintact skin, what occurs?
    a. incubation   c. replication
    b. contamination   d. immunization   _____

17. Which of the following is a basic bacterial shape?
    a. concave   c. spiral
    b. twist   d. oblong   _____

18. A bacilli bacterium is which of the following shapes?
    a. square   c. round
    b. spiral   d. rod   _____

19. Which of the following statements about bacteria is NOT true?
    a. all bacteria are bad because they infect living organisms
    b. an endospore is a rod-shaped bacterium's resting stage
    c. the slimy substance surrounding a bacterium cell is called a
       capsule
    d. bacterial spores resist heat, drying, and disinfectants   _____

20. Which of the following organisms grow on or in people for
    nourishment?
    a. viruses   c. parasites
    b. fungi   d. bacteria   _____

21. All of the following are true of viruses EXCEPT that they are:
    a. composed of cells   c. smaller than bacteria
    b. invisible to the naked eye   d. able to cause disease   _____

22. Viruses cause all of the following EXCEPT:
    a. hepatitis B   c. tuberculosis
    b. HIV   d. common cold   _____

23. Arthropods are an example of which of the following types of
    organism?
    a. viruses   c. fungi
    b. bacteria   d. parasites   _____

24. Which of the following entities starts the chain of infection?
    a. susceptible host   c. portal of entry
    b. infectious agent   d. reservoir   _____

25. All of the following are examples of infectious agents EXCEPT:
    a. blood   c. fungus
    b. virus   d. parasite   _____

26. In the chain of infection, a "hangout" where an infectious agent
    can live is called a(n):
    a. susceptible host   c. reservoir
    b. portal of exit   d. portal of entry   _____

27. In the chain of infection, which of the following is NOT an
    example of a portal of exit?
    a. nonintact skin   c. mouth mucous membrane
    b. work surface   d. acne lesion   _____

28. To reduce the likelihood that an infectious agent will leave a
    reservoir via a portal of exit, the esthetician should do all of the
    following EXCEPT:
    a. dispose of wastes properly   c. practice sharps safety
    b. wash hands appropriately   d. leave wounds uncovered   _____

29. In the chain of infection, an infectious agent gets from an old
    "hangout" to a new one via which of the following?
    a. portal of entry   c. mode of transmission
    b. susceptible host   d. portal of exit   _____

30. When an esthetician touches a client and an infectious agent is
    transferred, what is the mode of transmission?
    a. direct contact   c. airborne
    b. indirect contact   d. vectorborne   _____

31. Which of the following means for controlling modes of
    transmission is considered the most effective?
    a. disinfection of equipment
    b. proper hand-washing technique
    c. environmental control measures
    d. appropriate barrier use   _____

32. When they allow infectious agents to enter their new "hangouts,"
    acne lesions, unhealed tattoos, and percutaneous injuries are
    considered:
    a. modes of transmission   c. portals of entry
    b. reservoirs   d. susceptible hosts   _____

33. All measures that are taken to prevent infectious transmission by reducing the number of microorganisms are called:
    a. autoclave
    b. sharps
    c. germicide
    d. asepsis   _____

34. In the ABCs of infection control, the *B* stands for:
    a. bloodborne
    b. body hygiene
    c. biohazard
    d. bacteria   _____

35. All of the following are examples of medical asepsis EXCEPT:
    a. sterilization of equipment
    b. decontamination of tools
    c. preprocedure skin preparation
    d. proper hand-washing technique   _____

36. The foundation of aseptic technique is:
    a. cleanliness
    b. decontamination
    c. separation
    d. resolution   _____

37. Which of the following processes uses a physical or chemical procedure to destroy all forms of microbial life, including highly resistant bacterial spores?
    a. pathogenesis
    b. incubation
    c. sterilization
    d. disinfection   _____

38. In the esthetics workplace, antimicrobial soaps and skin preparations like prewaxing and postwaxing toners are examples of:
    a. decontaminants
    b. antiseptics
    c. antibiotics
    d. all answers   _____

39. The esthetician who follows proper technique uses antiseptic solutions to:
    a. replace hand washing
    b. cleanse visibly soiled hands
    c. sterilize equipment
    d. follow casual client contact   _____

40. Which of the following statements about soap is true?
    a. excessive use of antimicrobial soap can destroy the skin's resident flora
    b. plain soap kills the resident microorganisms of the skin
    c. antimicrobial soaps should be used every two to three hours
    d. none of these   _____

41. To execute proper hand-washing technique, the esthetician should rinse the hands:
    a. from the fingertips to the wrists
    b. palms first, then fingertips
    c. outward from thumbs to pinky fingers
    d. from the top of the wrists to the fingertips _____

42. All of the following are key points of hand washing EXCEPT:
    a. use lotion throughout the day
    b. always use warm water
    c. always rub the hands dry
    d. keep fingernails unpolished _____

43. Which of the following is a nonallergenic response of a natural rubber latex (NRL) allergy?
    a. Type IV hypersensitivity
    b. irritant dermatitis
    c. contact dermatitis
    d. Type I hypersensitivity _____

44. Which of the following reactions of natural rubber latex (NRL) allergy is the result of improper hand-washing technique?
    a. allergic contact dermatitis
    b. Type I hypersensitivity
    c. irritant dermatitis
    d. Type IV hypersensitivity _____

45. Which of the following common glove materials exhibits good puncture resistance but poor resistance to most organic solvents?
    a. polyvinyl chloride
    b. nitrile
    c. chloroprene
    d. thermoplastic elastomer _____

46. The glove-testing method that allows researchers to predict the effort wearers will exert to perform certain tasks is:
    a. tensile strength
    b. water leak
    c. ultimate elongation
    d. resistance to movement or stress _____

47. All of the following are characteristics of glove breakdown EXCEPT:
    a. cracking
    b. softening
    c. darkening
    d. tackiness _____

48. An esthetician with good personal hygiene does all of the following EXCEPT:
    a. don minimal jewelry
    b. wear long fingernails
    c. avoid heavy fragrance use
    d. cover or pull back the hair _____

49. Once equipment is rinsed, what is the next step in a sterilization process?
    a. thoroughly scrub to remove gross debris
    b. inspect for residual debris
    c. place in a disinfecting tub
    d. pat dry with a paper towel   _____

50. Which of the following processes removes or reduces contamination by infectious organisms or other harmful substances?
    a. cleaning   c. incubation
    b. disinfection   d. decontamination   _____

51. In the cleaning process, gross debris is removed as soon as possible to accomplish all of the following EXCEPT:
    a. minimize damage to devices
    b. limit the amount of nutrient material
    c. expose more surface area
    d. reduce the microorganisms   _____

52. Dead organisms in debris left on implements and equipment can:
    a. cause foreign body reactions
    b. impede an instrument's ability to function
    c. provide a breeding place for infectious agents
    d. all answers   _____

53. Which of the following statements is true?
    a. you can clean without disinfecting
    b. you can disinfect without cleaning
    c. you can sterilize without cleaning
    d. all answers   _____

54. The level of decontamination an item requires depends on the item's:
    a. manufacturer   c. size
    b. last use   d. material   _____

55. Which of the following statements about detergents is NOT true?
    a. those with a high pH are acidic
    b. they lower an object's surface tension
    c. they keep soils and dirt clumps in suspension
    d. those with a neutral pH are preferred for most cleaning   _____

56. Which of the following statements about lubrication is NOT true?
    a. lubrication solution resembles milk
    b. it is performed after cleaning
    c. it enhances instrument integrity
    d. it decreases an instrument's shelf life   ____

57. As instruments used on clients, all of the following are examples of critical items EXCEPT:
    a. tattoo needles   c. work surfaces
    b. comedo extractors   d. piercing needles   ____

58. Which level of disinfectants kills vegetative microorganisms, fungi, and small viruses but not necessarily bacterial spores?
    a. low   c. high
    b. intermediate   d. ultra   ____

59. On packages of esthetics materials, labels should include all of the following EXCEPT:
    a. packager's employee number
    b. description of package contents
    c. initials of package assembler
    d. date of sterilization   ____

60. In the steam sterilization process, pressure is needed to:
    a. compress the items into the package
    b. raise the water temperature above boiling
    c. provide a better environment for relative humidity
    d. all answers   ____

61. Indicators and integrators are both examples of which kind of monitoring?
    a. mechanical   c. metaphysical
    b. biological   d. chemical   ____

62. In general, spore tests should be run a minimum of how frequently?
    a. weekly   c. monthly
    b. biweekly   d. annually   ____

63. In the event of a sharps stick, the esthetician should screen for all of the following EXCEPT:
    a. workplace   c. severity
    b. employee   d. source   ____

64. Which of the following is NOT a key factor in glove selection?
    a. products to be used
    b. client body type
    c. treatment duration
    d. client/technician sensitivities ____

65. When visited by an Occupational Safety and Health Administration (OSHA) inspector, the esthetician should do all of the following EXCEPT:
    a. answer truthfully
    b. remain calm
    c. volunteer information
    d. document the visit ____

CHAPTER 3—ADVANCED HISTOLOGY OF THE CELL AND SKIN

1. In cellular function, the role of blood is to:
   a. give the cell membrane structure
   b. sandwich water in the cell membrane
   c. provide a barrier against the cell
   d. carry waste away from the cell   _____

2. Selective permeability allows a cell to:
   a. let choice substances in and out
   b. achieve more specialized function
   c. form distinct membrane layers
   d. all answers   _____

3. The role of receptors in a cell is to:
   a. serve as the "construction division"
   b. act as the cell's nutritionist
   c. communicate with other cells and tissues
   d. move substances from place to place   _____

4. Which of the following cell structures help build protein structures from a set of genetic instructions?
   a. lysosomes
   b. ribosomes
   c. mitochondria
   d. vacuoles   _____

5. Which of the following is NOT a job function of the mitochondria?
   a. store proteins for later conversion
   b. convert oxygen to carbon dioxide
   c. control water entering the cytoplasm
   d. convert oxygen and nutrients   _____

6. Which of the following cell components is responsible for manufacturing adenosine triphosphate (ATP)?
   a. lysosomes   c. mitochondria
   b. Golgi apparatus   d. endoplasmic reticulum   _____

7. All of the following are roles of the vacuoles EXCEPT:
   a. maintain the cell's correct pH
   b. isolate harmful materials
   c. store waste and excess food supplies
   d. create ribosome components   _____

8. Which of the following statements about the nucleus is NOT true?
   a. chromatin in the nucleus is made of nucleic acids
   b. protein fibers in the nucleus are responsible for cellular division
   c. its main component is protein
   d. cellular division in the nucleus yields two daughter cells ____

9. Which of the following cell types is found in the epidermis but not the dermis?
   a. keratinocyte   c. lymphocyte
   b. Langerhans   d. fibroblast ____

10. The period needed for cells to move through the epidermis is known as:
    a. differentiation period   c. action potential
    b. transit time   d. efferent window ____

11. Which of the following is a function of the skin?
    a. provide sexual attraction   c. produce vitamin C
    b. release body moisture   d. all answers ____

12. Through the process of differentiation, the keratinocyte becomes what kind of cell at the epidermis's surface?
    a. stem   c. mother
    b. corneum   d. corneocyte ____

13. Which of the following is NOT a function of the cytoskeleton?
    a. produce cell melanin   c. provide cell shape
    b. support the cell   d. move cell organelles ____

14. Of the fibers found in the cytoskeleton, which separate chromosomes during cellular division?
    a. intermediate filaments   c. microtubules
    b. microfilaments   d. neurofilaments ____

15. The intermediate filament that is found in the skin and hair and makes up most of the corneocyte is:
    a. vimentin   c. neurofilament
    b. keratin   d. desmosome ____

16. In the keratinocyte repair process, which of the following activates the fibroblasts and turns off the keratinocyte activation process?
    a. K6   c. EGF
    b. IL-I   d. TGF-B ____

17. The production of melanin is a complicated process known as:
    a. melanogenesis
    c. melanoma
    b. metastasis
    d. mesenchyme
    _____

18. In the melanin production process, melanin travels to the dendrites where it forms spheres called:
    a. eumelanins
    c. metastases
    b. melanosomes
    d. pheomelanins
    _____

19. Which of the following skin-lightening agents has been moved to prescription drug status given its side effects?
    a. arbutin
    c. hydroquinone
    b. ascorbic acid
    d. phytic acid
    _____

20. In Langerhans cells, which of the following look like tiny tennis rackets?
    a. multivesicular bodies
    c. lysosomes
    b. vesicles
    d. Birbeck granules
    _____

21. It is NOT accurate to say that Birbeck granules:
    a. participate in the cutaneous immune response
    b. function as antigen-presenting cells
    c. lack surface receptors for communication
    d. have faint striations and dark centers
    _____

22. Which of the following cells in the dermis are often star-shaped with many long cytoplasmic projections?
    a. fibroblasts
    c. mast cells
    b. keratinocytes
    d. melanocytes
    _____

23. Fibroblasts manufacture all of the following substances EXCEPT:
    a. reticulin
    c. collagen
    b. melanin
    d. elastin
    _____

24. A fibroblast that differentiates into an osteoblast becomes which of the following?
    a. cartilage
    c. muscle
    b. tendons
    d. bone
    _____

25. Which of the following statements about mast cells is NOT true?
    a. they have multiple nuclei
    b. they are involved in allergic reactions
    c. their granules contain histamine
    d. almost any connective tissue contains them
    _____

26. Which of the following types of cell is active in such immunological reactions as allergies and asthma?
    a. neutrophil
    c. eosinophil
    b. hydrophil
    d. basophil ____

27. Which of the following white blood cells stains a dark blue?
    a. eosinophil
    c. erythrophil
    b. basophil
    d. neutrophil ____

28. Neutrophils kill with oxygen in a process known as:
    a. respiratory burst
    c. cytokinesis
    b. chemotaxis
    d. active transport ____

29. Which of the following statements about neutrophils is NOT true?
    a. they are phagocytes that live in the blood
    b. they contain enzymes to kill bacteria
    c. they are the most common cell in the bloodstream
    d. they have a very long life span ____

30. Which of the following statements about eosinophils is true?
    a. they make up 70% of all white blood cells
    b. they are larger than neutrophils
    c. they can survive for two to three days
    d. in the skin they are a sign of rejuvenation ____

31. All of the following initiate replacement of the stratum corneum EXCEPT:
    a. rubbing
    c. sunburn
    b. moisturizing
    d. abrasion ____

32. In keratinocyte differentiation, which of the following cell types move up the epidermis to become stratum corneum cells?
    a. transient amplifying
    c. keratohyaline granule
    b. desmosome
    d. keratinocytoblast ____

33. What keratins are found in palmar skin?
    a. 5 and 14
    c. 1 and 9
    b. 2e and 10
    d. 1 and 10 ____

34. In the extracellular matrix (ECM), collagen and elastin belong in which major class of biomolecule?
    a. specialized
    c. anchoring
    b. proteoglycan
    d. structural ____

35. In collagen production, all of the following occur in the
    extracellular space EXCEPT:
    a. cutting of fibrils' terminal peptide ends
    b. forming of triple helix structure
    c. assembly of fibrils into microfibrils
    d. aggregation of cross-linked microfibrils   ____

36. Of the types of elastin-like fibers in dermal tissue, which contains
    only microfibrils?
    a. oxytalan   c. proline
    b. elaunin   d. elastic   ____

37. Which of the following proteoglycans is most common?
    a. keratin sulfate   c. dermatan sulfate
    b. chondroitin sulfate   d. heparan sulfate   ____

38. Versican is produced by which of the following?
    a. fibroblasts   c. epithelial cells
    b. smooth muscle cells   d. all answers   ____

39. Which of the following is NOT a function of small glycoprotein
    molecules like laminins, fribronectin, and tenascins?
    a. cell communication
    b. cell migration
    c. cell adhesion
    d. intercellular communication   ____

40. At which stage of the cell cycle are two sets of chromosomes
    checked?
    a. G_2 c. G_0
    b. S   d. M   ____

41. Which of the following substances blocks a cell's entry into the
    S phase?
    a. CdK   c. p53
    b. p27   d. MPF   ____

42. The aging process, which is usually characterized by the loss of
    some functional capacity, is known as:
    a. gastrulation   c. senescence
    b. acanthosis   d. homeostasis   ____

43. The study of the very early stages of development after
    fertilization is called:
    a. morphology   c. cytokinesis
    b. necrosis   d. embryology   ____

44. A ball-shaped layer of cells surrounding a fluid- or yolk-filled cavity is known as a:
   a. gastrula
   b. blastula
   c. zygote
   d. ectoderm
   _____

45. What occurs during the cleavage stage of embryo development?
   a. zygote rapidly divides
   b. egg is fertilized
   c. cells migrate inside the blastula
   d. cells surround a fluid cavity
   _____

46. Of the germ layers formed during gastrulation, which produces bones, the heart, and major blood vessels?
   a. blastoderm
   b. ectoderm
   c. mesoderm
   d. endoderm
   _____

47. Most of the central nervous system, including the brain, spinal cord, and motor neurons, form from which of the following?
   a. mesoderm
   b. neural crest
   c. endoderm
   d. neural tube
   _____

48. Of the basic types of body tissues, which is used to transport signals to other organs?
   a. epithelial
   b. nervous
   c. connective
   d. muscle
   _____

49. Which of the following types of muscle tissue is responsible for the voluntary muscle contraction that is used mainly to move the body?
   a. smooth
   b. cardiac
   c. skeletal
   d. all answers
   _____

50. Any material that elicits an immune response is called a(n):
   a. antigen
   b. cytokine
   c. dendrite
   d. antibody
   _____

51. Which of the following statements about T cells is NOT true?
   a. the *T* in T cell stands for thymus
   b. negative selection selects T cells that cannot recognize MHC molecules
   c. T cells form in the bone marrow
   d. none of these
   _____

52. In the humoral system, which type of cell causes cell lysis?
   a. memory
   b. suppressor
   c. helper
   d. cytotoxic
   _____

53. Which of the following types of junction occur at the top of the cell and possibly serve in some cell communication?
    a. gap
    b. adherens
    c. tight
    d. loose
    ____

54. In desmosome, the projections extending from the plaques are called:
    a. connexin
    b. desmocollins
    c. plaques
    d. desmoplakin
    ____

55. Which of the following statements is NOT true?
    a. charged compounds enter the skin easily
    b. liquid compounds penetrate faster than water-soluble ones
    c. daily soap use is deleterious for the skin barrier
    d. hairy body areas are good sites for skin penetration
    ____

CHAPTER 4—HORMONES

1. In essence, hormones serve the body as:
   a. protein substitutes
   b. chemical messengers
   c. substance passageways
   d. all answers _____

2. Which of the following is a role of the hypothalamus?
   a. regulate blood sugar or glucose levels
   b. create hormones for nerve impulses
   c. regulate calcium in the blood
   d. control some involuntary muscles _____

3. Which of the following is NOT a role of the pituitary gland?
   a. regulate the fluid retained by the body
   b. produce the hormones that control growth
   c. help digest foods taken in by the body
   d. cause the female breast to produce milk _____

4. Because it causes glands in the sex organs to produce sex hormones, follicle-stimulating hormone (FSH) is considered what type of hormone?
   a. endocrine
   b. trophic
   c. luteinizing
   d. exocrine _____

5. Corticoids do all of the following EXCEPT:
   a. produce growth hormones
   b. achieve water balance
   c. maintain sodium levels
   d. help regulate metabolism _____

6. The gland that is found in the abdomen is the:
   a. adrenal
   b. thyroid
   c. pineal
   d. pancreas _____

7. The ovaries are connected to the uterus by which of the following?
   a. vas deferens
   b. urethra
   c. fallopian tubes
   d. scrotum _____

8. The strongest of the estrogenic hormones produced by the ovaries is:
   a. estriol
   b. endocrine
   c. estrone
   d. estradiol _____

9. Which of the following hormones helps enlarge the pelvic opening during childbirth?
   a. luteinizing hormone
   b. relaxin
   c. progesterone
   d. follicle-stimulating hormone _____

10. Which of the following statements about puberty is true?
    a. females may reach puberty sooner than males
    b. sex glands have sexual function before puberty
    c. it generally begins around age 16
    d. androgens produced during puberty cause breasts in females   ____

11. In males, androgen production at puberty gives rise to all of the following EXCEPT:
    a. body hair   c. fatty hip deposits
    b. deeper voices   d. broader shoulders   ____

12. Which of the following statements about facial changes during puberty is NOT true?
    a. increased sebaceous gland activity renders pores visible
    b. the chin is the first part of the face to show pores
    c. small children have no easily visible pores
    d. none of these   ____

13. Which of the following is a recommended facial procedure for teenage clients?
    a. use a mild, antiacne product once weekly, if needed
    b. apply moisturizer twice daily
    c. use sunscreen sparingly to avoid breakouts
    d. follow cleansing with a mild toner   ____

14. In the salon, what is the first step in a teenager's facial treatment?
    a. cleanse with a cleansing milk
    b. presoften with a desincrustant solution
    c. apply a toner or an astringent
    d. use a light hydrating fluid   ____

15. Which of the following treatments is recommended for keratosis pilaris?
    a. use mildly abrasive scrubs
    b. conduct a light extraction
    c. apply 10% glycolic gel once daily
    d. all answers   ____

16. In which phase of the menstrual cycle does estrogen reach a high point, signaling the pituitary gland to release a large amount of luteinizing hormone (LH)?
    a. two   c. five
    b. three   d. six   ____

17. The thick layer of hormone-producing cells that serves as the nutrient, oxygen, and waste exchange system between a growing embryo and the mother's blood system is the:
    a. placenta
    c. trophoblast
    b. endometrium
    d. menarche ____

18. During pregnancy, telangiectasias are the result of:
    a. rapid weight gain
    c. increased blood flow
    b. excessive sun exposure
    d. pressure on the legs ____

19. Which of the following treatments is considered safe for pregnant women without a physician's approval?
    a. galvanic therapy
    c. electrolysis
    b. body massage
    d. all answers ____

20. To help alleviate the symptoms of premenstrual syndrome (PMS), women should avoid which of the following?
    a. aerobic workouts
    c. massage
    b. esthetic care
    d. tight-fitting clothing ____

21. Which of the following statements about premenstrual syndrome (PMS) and acne flare-ups is NOT true?
    a. it should be treated like any other acne
    b. many PMS acne flares fail to develop into pustules
    c. most PMS flares occur on the forehead
    d. it typically occurs seven to ten days before menstruation ____

22. Birth control pills that contain mainly progesterone work by:
    a. preventing the egg's maturation
    b. thickening the uterine fluids
    c. speeding the ovulation rate
    d. all answers ____

23. A woman on birth control pills who presents with a splotchy, pigmented complexion likely is experiencing:
    a. hyperpigmentation
    c. formication
    b. keratosis
    d. menarche ____

24. During menopause, it is accurate to say that the ovaries:
    a. release excess estrogen
    c. secrete FSH and LH
    b. overproduce follicles
    d. stop releasing ova ____

25. A client who presents with severe facial hyperpigmentation, dark freckles on the torso, and hyperpigmentation of the palms likely has:
    a. hypothyroidism
    c. Cushing's syndrome
    b. Addison's disease
    d. hyperthyroidism ____

CHAPTER 5—ANATOMY AND PHYSIOLOGY: MUSCLES AND NERVES

1. The role of myofilaments is to:
   a. help muscles contract and shorten
   b. regulate cardiac contractions
   c. push substances through smooth muscle
   d. striate smooth and skeletal muscle   _____

2. Cardiac muscles differ from other muscle types in that they:
   a. contract involuntarily   c. exhibit striations
   b. are the largest in size   d. all answers   _____

3. Muscle fibers that have single nuclei, lack striations, and achieve involuntary movement would be classified as:
   a. cardiac   c. rough
   b. smooth   d. skeletal   _____

4. Which of the following muscle types is a key contributor to the shape of the human form?
   a. cardiac   c. striated
   b. smooth   d. skeletal   _____

5. In skeletal muscle, several fibers are bunched together and wrapped in a fibrous sheathing called a(n):
   a. perimysium   c. epimysium
   b. endomysium   d. aponeurosis   _____

6. In the body, tendons serve to:
   a. connect nerves and muscle
   b. attach muscle to bone
   c. wrap several muscle fibers
   d. link bone to bone   _____

7. Irritability is the ability of muscle fibers to do which of the following?
   a. rotate clockwise   c. respond to stimuli
   b. oppose an action   d. move side to side   _____

8. Which of the following substances is classified as a neurotransmitter?
   a. endomysium   c. brachialis
   b. palpebra   d. acetylcholine   _____

9. Which of the following types of body movement reflects rotation of the arm?
   a. flexation
   b. supination
   c. adduction
   d. dorsiflexion
   _____

10. In its lower middle, the frontalis blends into which of the following?
   a. procerus
   b. obicularis oculi
   c. corrugator
   d. aponeurosis
   _____

11. When the upper eyelid raises to expose the orb of the eye, which of the following muscles is responsible?
   a. levator labii superioris
   b. orbicularis oculi
   c. levator palpebrae superioris
   d. corrugator supercilii
   _____

12. All of the following are muscles found around the mouth EXCEPT:
   a. risorius
   b. mentalis
   c. buccinator
   d. zygomaticus
   _____

13. The quadratus labii superioris is found _____ the mouth.
   a. above
   b. below
   c. inside
   d. around
   _____

14. The broad sheet of muscle that extends from the side of the nasolabial furrow and can convey contempt is the:
   a. orbicularis oris
   b. quadratus labii superior
   c. levator labii inferioris
   d. levator anguli oris
   _____

15. The orbicularis oculi is considered a(n) _____ muscle because it contracts to close an opening: the eye.
   a. orifice
   b. lateral
   c. sphincter
   d. antagonist
   _____

16. A person who wrinkles the chin while pouting uses which of the following muscles?
   a. levator labii inferioris
   b. buccinator
   c. depressor labii inferioris
   d. zygomaticus
   _____

17. The muscle that draws up the nose and down the central brow area is the:
   a. frenulum
   b. platysma
   c. buccinator
   d. procerus
   _____

18. The muscles responsible for flexing and rotating the head are the:
    a. pectorals   c. intercostals
    b. sternocleidomastoids   d. lastissimuses   _____

19. "Dual headed" muscles like sternocleidomastoids are broad:
    a. in their middles   c. at their points of origin
    b. when under stress   d. all answers   _____

20. People are able to support and balance their upright heads thanks
    to the muscle known as the:
    a. platysma   c. thorax
    b. intercostal   d. trapezius   _____

21. Which of the following types of muscle holds the urinary and
    digestive systems in place?
    a. anterior   c. abdominal
    b. pectoral   d. intercostal   _____

22. Which of the following forms the outermost layer of abdominal
    muscle?
    a. traverse abdominals   c. external obliques
    b. internal obliques   d. rectus abdominus   _____

23. Of the posterior muscles of the trunk, which compose most of the
    muscle tissue of the lower back?
    a. platysma   c. trapezius
    b. latissimus dorsal   d. erector spinae   _____

24. Which of the major muscles in the arm flexes the elbow from its
    origin point at the deltoid muscle?
    a. brachialis   c. deltoid
    b. bicep brachii   d. triceps brachii   _____

25. All of the following regulate hip movement EXCEPT:
    a. extensors   c. rotators
    b. adductors   d. flexors   _____

26. Which member of the gluteus group of muscles is designed
    primarily for hip rotation?
    a. gluteus maximus   c. brachialis
    b. gluteus medius   d. brevis   _____

27. The adductor group of muscles does NOT include the adductor:
    a. magnus   c. medius
    b. brevis   d. longus   _____

28. All of the following are responsible for dorsiflexion of the ankle EXCEPT:
    a. soleus
    b. tertius peroneus
    c. peroneus longus
    d. peroneus brevis _____

29. Of the branches of the external carotid/temporal artery, which splits off at the angle of the jaw and initially runs beneath the lower jaw?
    a. transverse facial
    b. external maxillary
    c. anterior temporal
    d. facial frontal _____

30. All of the following are branches of the trigeminal nerve EXCEPT:
    a. maxillary
    b. mandibular
    c. facial
    d. ophthalmic _____

CHAPTER 6—ANATOMY AND PHYSIOLOGY: THE CARDIOVASCULAR AND LYMPHATIC SYSTEMS

1. Smoking contributes to the desiccation or _____ of the capillaries.
    a. drying
    b. splitting
    c. cleansing
    d. clogging   ____

2. During an average lifetime, the heart pumps approximately how much blood?
    a. 2 million tankers
    b. 1 million barrels
    c. 500,000 gallons
    d. 250,000 pints   ____

3. Blood flow and temperature is regulated by a delicate balancing process called:
    a. circulation
    b. desiccation
    c. homeostasis
    d. hypoxia   ____

4. It is accurate to say that white blood cells:
    a. fail to circulate in the blood
    b. are smaller than red blood cells
    c. change shape to navigate capillaries
    d. all answers   ____

5. Which of the following statements about blood is true?
    a. it has solid and liquid properties only
    b. it is slightly cooler than the body
    c. it composes about 25% of body weight
    d. it is a circulating connective tissue   ____

6. The yellowish, liquid component of blood is known as:
    a. albumin
    b. plasma
    c. neutrophil
    d. plexus   ____

7. All of the following are waste products found in blood EXCEPT:
    a. glucose
    b. uric acid
    c. urea
    d. lactic acid   ____

8. Which of the following plasma contents carried in blood assist osmotic pressure and aid in the hydration of muscles and nerves?
    a. antibodies
    b. hormones
    c. electrolytes
    d. nutrients   ____

9. Which of the following statements about erythrocytes, or red blood cells, is true?
   a. they are multinucleate
   b. they accomplish gas transfer
   c. they are more robust than other cells
   d. they can exit and reenter the bloodstream   _____

10. All of the following are types of granulocytes EXCEPT:
    a. neutrophils   c. basophils
    b. eosinophils   d. monocytes   _____

11. Which of the following leukocytes become macrophages to aid in overall systemic waste removal?
    a. monocytes   c. basophils
    b. neutrophils   d. lymphocytes   _____

12. All of the following are types of anemia EXCEPT:
    a. aplastic   c. sickle cell
    b. hemolytic   d. aortic valve   _____

13. The condition that results in oxygen deficiency due to defective hemoglobin cells is:
    a. hemophilia   c. thalassemia
    b. pericarditis   d. leukemia   _____

14. The heart attaches to surrounding organs via the:
    a. myocardium   c. pericardium
    b. epicardium   d. endocardium   _____

15. The contraction of the heart is known as:
    a. arrhythmia   c. diastole
    b. systole   d. aneurysm   _____

16. Which of the following is true of pulmonary circulation?
    a. the right atrium sends blood to the right ventricle
    b. the left ventricle pumps blood into the body
    c. the left atrium receives oxygenated blood
    d. all answers   _____

17. The valve that prevents backflow between the left atrium and left ventricle is the:
    a. tricuspid   c. semilunar
    b. pulmonary   d. bicuspid   _____

18. Arteries that are tortuous are:
    a. very painful
    b. extremely short
    c. highly curved
    d. very branched   _____

19. Networks of intersecting venules are known as:
    a. plexuses
    b. ligatures
    c. systoles
    d. none of these   _____

20. Which of the following statements about the lymphatic system is NOT true?
    a. it cleans up after the circulatory system
    b. edema can result when lymphatic vessels fail to function
    c. lymphatic vessels reabsorb lymph from the blood
    d. lymphatic drainage can worsen areas of inflammation   _____

CHAPTER 7—CHEMISTRY AND BIOCHEMISTRY

1. All of the following are examples of elements EXCEPT:
   - a. oxygen
   - b. silver
   - c. light
   - d. gold _____

2. Which of the following statements about chemistry is NOT true?
   - a. negatively charged electrons orbit an atom
   - b. the nucleus of an atom is positively charged
   - c. electrons far outweigh the much lighter protons
   - d. each atom of the same element is exactly alike _____

3. The weight of a chemical made of multiple elements is called the _____ weight.
   - a. composite
   - b. atomic
   - c. biochemical
   - d. molecular _____

4. The lightest and most abundant element in the universe is:
   - a. hydrogen
   - b. chlorine
   - c. oxygen
   - d. carbon _____

5. Which of the following elements has the lowest atomic weight?
   - a. oxygen
   - b. carbon
   - c. sodium
   - d. chlorine _____

6. Which of the following elements is a poisonous, pale green gas in its basic state?
   - a. chlorine
   - b. oxygen
   - c. carbon
   - d. sodium _____

7. In the periodic table of elements, the symbol for oxygen is:
   - a. O_2
   - b. Oxy
   - c. O
   - d. OO _____

8. Which of the following elements is needed by all animals, but not by plants?
   - a. hydrogen
   - b. sodium
   - c. carbon
   - d. chlorine _____

9. When carbon combines with oxygen and hydrogen, all of the following can result EXCEPT:
   - a. fats
   - b. sugars
   - c. celluloses
   - d. proteins _____

10. In a typical equation for a chemical reaction, the number that precedes each chemical represents the:
   a. number of molecules
   b. molecular weight
   c. number of atoms
   d. math function   _____

11. Because heat is needed to trigger some chemical reactions, it is considered a:
   a. reactant
   b. by-product
   c. catalyst
   d. control   _____

12. Which of the following is an example of a polymer?
   a. DNA
   b. sugars
   c. proteins
   d. all answers   _____

13. Which of the following amino acid chains are attached to fats?
   a. lipoproteins
   b. glycoproteins
   c. phosphoroproteins
   d. pleuroproteins   _____

14. The proteins that make up the blood and lymph are:
   a. scleroproteins
   b. globulins
   c. albumins
   d. all answers   _____

15. When using cosmetics, estheticians should do all of the following EXCEPT:
   a. apply premasks with slightly acidic pHs
   b. follow high-pH cleansers with low-pH toners
   c. use cosmetics with a slightly acidic pH
   d. adopt esthetic products with a pH of 3.0   _____

16. A mixture in which solute is dispersed evenly throughout the solvent is considered:
   a. distilled
   b. saturated
   c. hydrated
   d. homogeneous   _____

17. In chemical terms, the prefix *poly-* means:
   a. protein
   b. charged
   c. many
   d. linked   _____

18. Cocoa, berries, grapes, and French pine are all examples of:
   a. anthocyanidins
   b. proanthocyanidins
   c. flavonols
   d. xanthophylls   _____

19. Which of the following statements about fatty acids is true?
    a. unsaturated fats have lower melting points than saturated fats
    b. saturated fatty acids have extra double bonds
    c. polyunsaturated fats are more stable than monosaturated oils
    d. all answers   _____

20. Which of the following functional groups includes citral, citronellal, and neral as compounds?
    a. ester   c. phenol
    b. ketone   d. aldehyde   _____

CHAPTER 8—LASER, LIGHT ENERGY, AND RADIO-FREQUENCY THERAPY

1. Which of the following occurs when tissue is ablated?
   a. vaporization
   b. regeneration
   c. obstruction
   d. attenuation
   _____

2. Which of the following parties is responsible for creating the first visible laser?
   a. Albert Einstein
   b. Arthur Schawlow
   c. Theodore Maiman
   d. Charles Townes
   _____

3. The acronym LASER stands for which of the following?
   a. limited allowance for some electronic rays
   b. light amplification by the stimulated emission of radiation
   c. low accommodation source for emitting radiation
   d. light allowance seen when equilibrating rays
   _____

4. The electromagnetic spectrum of radiation includes all of the following types of light EXCEPT:
   a. invisible infrared
   b. visible
   c. invisible ultraviolet
   d. visible radiation
   _____

5. Which of the following statements about the electromagnetic spectrum of radiation is NOT true?
   a. invisible lasers have long-term harmful effects
   b. photons are small particles of energy
   c. penetration is directly related to wavelength size
   d. wavelengths are measured in nanometers
   _____

6. Which of the following types of light has all waves traveling in the same direction and in unison?
   a. monochromatic
   b. coherent
   c. collimated
   d. all answers
   _____

7. What is the name for a target in the epidermis or dermis that absorbs a laser beam's thermal energy?
   a. photon
   b. cytochrome
   c. nanometer
   d. chromophore
   _____

8. All of the following are common chromophores in the body EXCEPT:
   a. collagen
   b. water
   c. fat
   d. blood
   _____

9. Which of the following statements about cosmetic lasers is NOT true?
   a. dark pigment absorbs hair-removal lasers
   b. lasers that produce new collagen tend to be water absorbers
   c. vascular lasers seek melanin as their chromophore
   d. the target of tattoo lasers is specific dyes
   _____

10. When exposed to a client's skin, a laser spreads laterally due to the effect known as:
    a. scatter
    b. absorption
    c. reflection
    d. transmission

11. In the process of selective photothermolysis, a targeted chromophore does which of the following?
    a. enhances collagen synthesis
    b. selectively absorbs light
    c. loses most heat
    d. all answers

12. Irradiance multiplied by exposure time is known as:
    a. lysis
    b. power density
    c. spot size
    d. fluence

13. Which of the following is measured in watts/centimeter squared?
    a. pulse duration
    b. radiant energy
    c. power density
    d. spot size

14. One way to decrease fluence is to increase the:
    a. laser's diameter
    b. laser's energy output
    c. exposure time
    d. all answers

15. In which of the following cooling techniques is cold water circulated through a window on the laser head?
    a. chilled tip
    b. parallel cooling
    c. cryogen spray
    d. forced air

16. Which of the following agencies classifies medical devices according to their potential degrees of hazard?
    a. Food and Drug Administration
    b. International Electrotechnical Commission
    c. American National Standards Institute
    d. Occupational Safety and Health Administration

17. According to the U.S. Food and Drug Administration (FDA), many light and energy devices that estheticians use fall into which class?
    a. I
    b. II
    c. III
    d. IV

18. A professional whose duties include hazard classification of all laser systems and control measures to reduce the risk of injury from lasers is called a:
    a. safety hazard monitor
    b. laser oversight manager
    c. laser ambassador
    d. laser safety officer

19. According to American National Standards Institute (ANSI) standards, which of the following is generally considered a Class II device?
    a. cosmetic laser
    b. laser pointer
    c. ophthalmic laser
    d. compact disc player ____

20. The nominal hazard zone (NHZ) describes which of the following?
    a. level of training zone below expert skill
    b. portion of the equipment in contact with the laser
    c. area of the face most at risk of injury
    d. room where skin or eye injury can occur ____

21. Which of the following can transmit lasers?
    a. eye fluids
    b. closed windows
    c. clear liquids
    d. all answers ____

22. Which part of the eye is the essential mechanism for magnification?
    a. cornea
    b. retina
    c. lens
    d. all answers ____

23. A method of blocking laser energy is:
    a. attenuation
    b. impedance
    c. lipolysis
    d. ablation ____

24. Which of the following is NOT an engineering control mandated by the Federal Center for Devices and Radiological Health (CDRH) for laser devices?
    a. emergency stop button
    b. laser key lock
    c. guarded foot switch
    d. HEPA filter ____

25. Which of the following responses targets blood vessels, darkening and coagulating them?
    a. vascular lesion
    b. pigmented lesion
    c. collagen stimulation
    d. none of these ____

26. In the pigmented-lesion response, which of the following is immediately evident?
    a. crusting
    b. erythema
    c. blanching
    d. darkening ____

27. Which of the following statements about photomechanical tissue response is NOT true?
    a. the healing period is approximately three weeks
    b. the impact area whitens without thermal damage
    c. pigment around the impact area remains intact
    d. tissue temperature rises 300°C in nanoseconds ____

28. All of the following laser wavelengths are associated with blue pigment dye absorption EXCEPT:
    a. Q-switched 532nm
    b. Q-switched 694nm Ruby
    c. Q-switched 755nm Alexandrite
    d. Q-switched 1064nm Nd:YAG

    _____

29. Fat removal, cellulite reduction, and body sculpting are all achieved by splitting or destroying fat cells, a process called:
    a. modulation   c. lipolysis
    b. attenuation   d. impedance

    _____

30. A smooth-beam laser is used for all of the following applications EXCEPT:
    a. acne scarring   c. collagen stimulation
    b. hair removal   d. wrinkle reduction

    _____

31. Which of the following is indicative of variable interpulse delay IPL devices?
    a. medium viscosity gels   c. adjustable pulse widths
    b. adjustable energy levels d. cooling between pulses

    _____

32. Which of the following types of energy is based on alternating energy waveforms that produce localized, nonspecific heat in the epidermis and dermis?
    a. light   c. optical
    b. radio frequency   d. all answers

    _____

33. What is the name for color-coded proteins in a cell's cytoplasm?
    a. cytochromes   c. joules
    b. watts   d. chromophores

    _____

Part 3: Skin Sciences

CHAPTER 9—NUTRITION AND STRESS MANAGEMENT

1. Which of the following statements about nutrients and diet is NOT true?
   a. carbohydrates are energy nutrients
   b. metabolism begins immediately upon ingestion
   c. anabolism builds tissue rather than breaks it down
   d. calories are part of every food   _____

2. Catabolism includes which of the following processes?
   a. anabolism   c. digestion
   b. metabolism   d. all answers   _____

3. A person who is aging would be expected to exhibit which of the following characteristics?
   a. increased caloric need   c. decreased body fat
   b. decreased bone mass   d. higher physical activity   _____

4. A deficiency of which of the following vitamins can cause alterations in hair growth?
   a. A   c. C
   b. B6   d. B9   _____

5. Vitamin B7 (biotin) is esthetically beneficial because it:
   a. maintains skin oil balance   c. slows skin aging
   b. speeds hair growth   d. controls hyperpigmentation _____

6. As they generally operate in the body, free radicals do which of the following?
   a. repair tissue   c. slow aging
   b. take electrons   d. prevent disease   _____

7. Antioxidants are able to neutralize free radicals because they can:
   a. split and create more electrons
   b. fight off electron attacks
   c. give electrons and remain stable
   d. all answers   _____

8. All of the following are good sources of antioxidants EXCEPT:
   a. fruit   c. whole grains
   b. red wine   d. coffee   _____

9. Diets rich in sugar are not recommended because they:
   a. deplete B vitamins
   b. raise blood pressure
   c. damage free radicals
   d. suppress immunity
   _____

10. A dietary lack of serotonin leads to which of the following?
    a. pain sensitivity
    b. restlessness
    c. poor mood
    d. agitation
    _____

11. Which of the following is an example of a neurotransmitter?
    a. norepinephrine
    b. serotonin
    c. both a and b
    d. neither a nor b
    _____

12. Which of the following is known to release stress hormones and create a state of agitation?
    a. fat
    b. caffeine
    c. sugar
    d. salt
    _____

13. All of the following are results of glycation EXCEPT:
    a. sagging skin
    b. hyperpigmentation
    c. stiff blood vessels
    d. stretchy organs
    _____

14. Glycation contributes to all of the following diseases EXCEPT:
    a. anorexia
    b. Alzheimer's disease
    c. heart disease
    d. cataracts
    _____

15. Which of the following has the lowest level of advanced glycation end products (AGEs)?
    a. cake
    b. cereal
    c. coffee
    d. tea
    _____

16. When seeking to reverse the effects of advanced glycation end products (AGEs), all of the following are recommended means of cooking EXCEPT:
    a. stewing
    b. broiling
    c. poaching
    d. boiling
    _____

17. A person with high advanced glycation end product (AGE) levels would likely eat a diet rich in all of the following foods EXCEPT:
    a. sausage
    b. French fries
    c. legumes
    d. cream cheese
    _____

18. Sensitivities and irritations tend to increase with stress because:
    a. cortisone secretions increase
    b. blood flow constricts
    c. cell turnover slows
    d. pores become blocked
    _____

19. When the body faces a threat, what is the role of cortisol?
    a. raise blood pressure
    b. elevate the heart rate
    c. trigger the adrenal glands
    d. release energy from fat cells   ____

20. All of the following are internal stress triggers EXCEPT:
    a. need for perfectionism   c. fear of job loss
    b. heavy traffic   d. anxiety about a test   ____

CHAPTER 10—ADVANCED SKIN DISORDERS: SKIN IN DISTRESS

1. In the inflammation cascade, the role of inflammatory mediators is to:
   a. break down skin substances
   b. release white blood cells
   c. alert the immune system
   d. signal other chemicals _____

2. Inflammation can be divided into what two categories?
   a. clinical and subclinical
   b. stage one and stage two
   c. superficial and deeper
   d. serious and minor _____

3. A wound that involves muscle and exposes bone is at stage:
   a. one
   b. two
   c. three
   d. four _____

4. Injuries that extend into the connective tissue of the dermis are categorized as:
   a. inflammatory
   b. deep
   c. proliferative
   d. superficial _____

5. For deep wounds, the first phase of healing is:
   a. maturation
   b. inflammatory
   c. regeneration
   d. proliferative _____

6. Which phase of the healing process features an increase in the vascularity of the wound?
   a. proliferative
   b. inflammatory
   c. maturation
   d. hemostasis _____

7. The control of bleeding that occurs during deep-wound healing is known as:
   a. exudation
   b. homeostasis
   c. hemostasis
   d. vasodilation _____

8. Healing by primary intention involves which of the following?
   a. approximating the wound margin
   b. minimizing granulation tissue
   c. accelerating wound healing
   d. all answers _____

9. Which of the following types of suture features interrupted single loops?
   a. simple
   b. buried
   c. running
   d. none of these _____

10. Which of the following types of suture requires removal?
    a. simple
    b. superficial
    c. running
    d. all answers

    _____

11. As aftercare products, dressings are applied to wounds to absorb exudates, which are:
    a. sutures
    b. fluids
    c. hairs
    d. scabs

    _____

12. As wound care, dressings are designed to do all of the following EXCEPT:
    a. reduce pain
    b. absorb exudates
    c. replace scabs
    d. guard against contaminants

    _____

13. Which of the following statements about bathing during the initial stages of would healing is true?
    a. long periods of water immersion help prevent infection
    b. in initial healing stages water absorption increases
    c. initially, the sebaceous glands produce more protective oils
    d. all answers

    _____

14. To best support the wound-healing process, a client should do which of the following?
    a. maintain adequate protein intake
    b. eliminate zinc from the diet
    c. limit vitamin A intake
    d. avoid foods with manganese

    _____

15. As aftercare products for wounds, silicone patches generally exhibit their results in:
    a. three to six months
    b. one to two months
    c. twenty-four hours
    d. twelve hours

    _____

16. Dark-brown patches of concentrated pigmentation on the hands and face are known as:
    a. dysplasia
    b. chalazia
    c. rosacea
    d. chloasma

    _____

17. A client who presents with white splotches on the chest and back likely has which of the following conditions?
    a. chloasma
    b. rhinophyma
    c. tinea versicolor
    d. hyperpigmentation

    _____

18. Most damage from the sun is sustained during which of the following periods?
    a. infancy to early childhood   c. early adulthood
    b. childhood and adolescence   d. late adulthood   _____

19. What process occurs when collagen and fibrils collapse from repeated sun exposure, causing the skin to collapse?
    a. cross-linking   c. interlocking
    b. hemostasis   d. none of these   _____

20. A client with sun-damaged skin will usually present with all of the following EXCEPT:
    a. dry patches   c. freckled areas
    b. nondistended capillaries   d. pronounced wrinkles   _____

21. Skin that grows abnormally would be classified as:
    a. exudate   c. perioral
    b. couperose   d. dysplasic   _____

22. An older client who presents with a large, flat, crusty-looking yellow-gray lesion on the face most likely has which of the following types of skin damage?
    a. solar freckles   c. seborrheic keratosis
    b. sebaceous hyperplasia   d. actinic keratosis   _____

23. The most common form of treatment for seborrheic keratoses is:
    a. curettage   c. conventional surgery
    b. cryosurgery   d. electrodesiccation   _____

24. A cell that has been programmed to die undergoes the process known as:
    a. dysplasia   c. chalazia
    b. hemostasis   d. apoptosis   _____

25. Which of the following occurs first when a cell is exposed to ultraviolet (UV) light?
    a. UV gets past melanin and damages the cell
    b. melanocytes send melanin to surrounding cells
    c. melanin situates between the UV and the nucleus
    d. none of these   _____

26. The second most common type of skin cancer is:
    a. squamous cell carcinoma   c. lentigenal carcinoma
    b. basal cell carcinoma   d. melanoma   _____

27. A client who presents with dark, molelike lesions most likely has which of the following types of skin cancer?
    a. basal cell carcinoma   c. erythema
    b. melanoma   d. squamous cell carcinoma   ____

28. In the ABCDEs of skin cancer, the *E* stands for:
    a. erythema   c. expanding
    b. elevated   d. evolving   ____

29. Which of the following statements about acne vulgaris is NOT true?
    a. it is the most common form of acne
    b. excess sebum is its cause
    c. it tends to present in adulthood
    d. all answers   ____

30. A client who is unable to shed and replace epidermal cells most likely has which of the following conditions?
    a. epidermal corneum
    b. actinic keratosis
    c. retention hyperkeratosis
    d. perifollicular inflammation   ____

31. Microcomedones result when which of the following occurs?
    a. sebum builds in the follicle's bottom
    b. cells push to the surface of the skin
    c. bacteria become visible on the skin
    d. all answers   ____

32. The opening of a follicle is called a(n):
    a. cytokine   c. flare
    b. ostium   d. exudate   ____

33. Which of the following is an example of an inflammatory lesion?
    a. blackhead   c. whitehead
    b. acne pimple   d. all answers   ____

34. A clump of white blood cells on the surface of the skin is called a:
    a. papule   c. pustule
    b. open comedone   d. closed comedone   ____

35. Acne at which grade has many deep cysts and scar formation?
    a. 1   c. 3
    b. 2   d. 4   ____

36. According to many researchers, all of the following parts of a woman's face respond well to male hormone sebaceous stimulation EXCEPT the:
   a. temples
   b. chin
   c. jawline
   d. lower cheeks
   _____

37. Hormonal acne differs from comedonal acne in that hormonal acne is:
   a. built up more slowly
   b. more inflammatory
   c. caused only by hormones
   d. all answers
   _____

38. A client who presents with skin that is red, irritated, and rough in patches, as well as dotted with small whiteheads, mostly likely has the condition known as:
   a. actinic keratosis
   b. perioral dermatitis
   c. seborrheic dermatitis
   d. keratosis pilaris
   _____

39. Of the subtypes of rosacea, which is characterized by diffuse facial redness and patchy redness on the nose and cheeks?
   a. papulopustular
   b. phymatous
   c. erythematotelangiectatic
   d. ocular
   _____

40. The esthetician should refer a client for medical evaluation when:
   a. blemishes or growths change
   b. skin rashes are undiagnosed
   c. spots are unrecognizable
   d. all answers
   _____

CHAPTER 11—SKIN TYPING AND AGING ANALYSIS

1. When assessing skin, the magnifying lamp determines all of the following EXCEPT:
   a. sun damage
   b. tissue elasticity
   c. visible conditions
   d. skin texture
   ____

2. Fitzpatrick skin typing allows the esthetician to do which of the following?
   a. measure the skin's tolerance to the sun
   b. predict the skin's response to treatments
   c. quantify the skin's amount of pigment
   d. all answers
   ____

3. According to the Fitzpatrick skin-typing scale, people with Type VI skin are typically of which descent?
   a. Mediterranean
   b. African
   c. English
   d. German
   ____

4. According to the Fitzpatrick skin-typing scale, a person with Type IV skin has what color skin?
   a. dark brown
   b. black
   c. brown
   d. white
   ____

5. When grading genetic disposition to determine a person's skin type, which of the following would earn two points?
   a. light-brown skin
   b. light-blue eyes
   c. brownish-black eyes
   d. naturally chestnut hair
   ____

6. When grading genetic disposition to determine skin type, what number of freckles earns the fewest points?
   a. many
   b. few
   c. several
   d. none
   ____

7. When grading skin for reaction to sun exposure, a person who tans very easily would earn how many points?
   a. one
   b. two
   c. three
   d. four
   ____

8. When grading for tanning habits, respondents would earn the most points for exposing their bodies to the sun or artificial sunlamps:
   a. over three months ago
   b. less than a month ago
   c. two to three months ago
   d. one to two months ago
   ____

9. A person with a total skin-type score of 32 is Fitzpatrick skin type:
   a. II
   b. III
   c. IV
   d. VI ___

10. Which of the following Fitzpatrick skin types is prone to showing hyperpigmentation from stimulating exfoliation treatments?
    a. I
    b. II
    c. III
    d. IV ___

11. Which of the following scales is used to evaluate the level of skin's sun damage based on wrinkling?
    a. Glogau
    b. Rubin
    c. Fitzpatrick
    d. isotype ___

12. On the Glogau scale, a client with which type of skin exhibits early-to-moderate photoaging and light keratosis?
    a. I
    b. II
    c. III
    d. IV ___

13. At which level of Rubin's classification of photodamage would a client benefit from laser resurfacing?
    a. 1
    b. 2
    c. 3
    d. 4 ___

14. On which level of Rubin's classification of photodamage are alterations to the epidermis only?
    a. 4
    b. 3
    c. 2
    d. 1 ___

15. According to the Kligman rosacea classification, a client who presents with which of the following should be referred to a physician?
    a. inflammation and pustules along the hairline and chin
    b. large nodules and orange-peel appearance
    c. skin that itches and burns in the presence of cosmetics
    d. erythema in the nasolabial folds and cheeks ___

16. The element in traditional Chinese medicine (TCM) that relates to venous circulation is:
    a. metal
    b. wood
    c. water
    d. fire ___

17. According to traditional Chinese medicine (TCM), which of the following skin conditions is associated with the earth element?
    a. oily hair
    b. red, irritated scalp
    c. pimples on the scalp
    d. limp hair ___

18. According to traditional Chinese medicine (TCM), the facial reflex zone for the spleen is the:
    a. frontal part of the neck   c. temples of the head
    b. area between the eyebrows   d. bridge of the nose   ____

19. It is NOT accurate to say that women of the estrogen isotype:
    a. carry their weight in the hips
    b. are generally larger boned
    c. have less-frequent breakouts
    d. are prone to autoimmune disorders   ____

20. Which of the following statements about the categories of estrogen isotypes is true?
    a. clients of the EX type seldom have terminal hair
    b. the EX category has the least estrogen
    c. the EY category has less visible pores
    d. clients of the EY type have narrower features   ____

CHAPTER 12—SKIN CARE PRODUCTS: INGREDIENTS AND CHEMISTRY

1. The study of biology helps researchers understand how:
    a. ingredients are mixed to produce products
    b. skin cells react to and absorb products
    c. drugs and chemicals affect the body's function
    d. all answers   _____

2. All of the following are roles of functional ingredients EXCEPT:
    a. prevent bacterial contamination
    b. determine a product's texture
    c. cause appearance changes
    d. regulate a product's pH   _____

3. According to the U.S. Federal Drug Administration (FDA), "articles
    intended to be rubbed, poured, sprinkled, or otherwise applied to
    the human body or any part thereof for cleansing, beautifying,
    promoting physical attractiveness, or altering the appearance" are
    considered:
    a. cosmetics   c. foods
    b. drugs   d. all answers   _____

4. When penicillin is delivered in a gelatin capsule, the gelatin of
    the capsule is considered what kind of ingredient?
    a. active   c. performance
    b. functional   d. inactive   _____

5. The phrase, "This product makes your skin stronger and suppler"
    is an example of what kind of claim?
    a. active   c. cosmetic
    b. drug   d. functional   _____

6. Which of the following categories of products are intended solely
    to benefit the skin in some way?
    a. cosmeceuticals   c. cosmetics
    b. drugs   d. preservatives   _____

7. As a cosmetics component, the role of the vehicle is to
    _____ the skin.
    a. keep substances from penetrating
    b. lower the surface tension of
    c. deliver ingredients to
    d. adhere powder cosmetics to   _____

8. Which of the following processes kills all bacteria, viruses, and spores in water?
   a. distillation
   c. deionization
   b. emulsification
   d. sterilization _____

9. As cosmetics components, protectants are designed to:
   a. prevent water evaporation
   c. remove trace elements
   b. spread other products
   d. lift away dead cells _____

10. One of the drawbacks of petrolatum as a vehicle or performance agent is that it:
    a. tends to cause allergic reactions
    b. has a highly greasy feel
    c. suspends little pigment
    d. lacks waterproofing _____

11. Because silicones helps powders stay in cake form and adhere to the skin, they are considered:
    a. functional vehicles
    c. web polymers
    b. performance ingredients
    d. pressing agents _____

12. Ingredients that fail to cross-react with natural skin-functioning reactions are considered:
    a. inactive ingredients
    c. biologically inert
    b. free radicals
    d. none of these _____

13. In clog- and acne-prone skin, the phenomenon known as retention hyperkeratosis causes which of the following?
    a. cell buildup in the follicles
    b. development of comedones
    c. biochemical inflammation
    d. creation of microshells _____

14. Because they do not irritate the insides of follicles, silicones can be classified as:
    a. defatting agents
    c. chelating agents
    b. non-acnegenic
    d. non-comedogenic _____

15. As an emollient, polyethylene is a wax derived from what type of source?
    a. animal
    c. plant
    b. synthetic
    d. petroleum _____

16. All of the following waxes derive from plant sources EXCEPT:
    a. candelilla
    c. carnauba
    b. jojoba
    d. lanolin _____

17. Which of the following statements about fatty acids is NOT true?
    a. they derive from plants or animals
    b. they are used as emollients
    c. they are corrosive to the skin
    d. they are used as performance ingredients

18. Which of the fatty acids used in skin-care and cosmetic formulations occurs naturally in many dairy products?
    a. palmitic
    b. lauric
    c. oleic
    d. stearic

19. A liquid that is very thick and pours slowly is said to have high:
    a. buffering
    b. viscosity
    c. gommage
    d. occlusivity

20. The fatty alcohol cetyl alcohol is used as a:
    a. product silkener
    b. foam booster
    c. superfatting agent
    d. cream thickener

21. Which of the following fatty esters is comedogenic and should be avoided for oily skin?
    a. isopropyl myristate
    b. isopropyl isostearate
    c. propylene glycol dicaprate
    d. glyceryl stearate

22. On a cosmetic product label, which of the following indicates an ingredient is an ester?
    a. letters *cone*
    b. prefix *sil-*
    c. suffix *-ate*
    d. letters *con*

23. As a cosmetics ingredient, a surfactant is designed to do which of the following?
    a. attract water
    b. lower surface tension
    c. prevent evaporation
    d. coat the skin

24. Which of the following types of surfactant has a negative ionic charge only?
    a. cationic
    b. amphoteric
    c. nonionic
    d. anionic

25. For sensitive and dry skin types, cosmetic manufacturers often add a fatty _____ to cut a surfactant's contact with the skin.
    a. acid
    b. oil
    c. wax
    d. all answers

26. In general, a cleanser for oily skin contains _____ surfactant than a cleanser for dry skin.
    a. more
    b. less
    c. the same
    d. b or c

    _____

27. Compounds that keep water and oil in uniform mixture are polymers of which length?
    a. short
    b. medium
    c. long
    d. none of these

    _____

28. In a water-and-oil mixture, the water is considered which of the following phases?
    a. suspended
    b. external
    c. surrounded
    d. internal

    _____

29. Because salad dressing is always separated and must be shaken, it is considered a(n):
    a. suspension
    b. polymer
    c. globule
    d. emulsion

    _____

30. Which of the following is an example of a gas emulsified in an external phase liquid?
    a. makeup
    b. mousse
    c. hairspray
    d. all answers

    _____

31. It is accurate to say that water-in-oil (w/o) emulsions tend to have:
    a. lighter textures
    b. lower weights
    c. more water
    d. more emulsifier

    _____

32. When water is added to powdered ice tea mix, the powdered mix is considered the:
    a. solvent
    b. emulsion
    c. solute
    d. globule

    _____

33. Cosmetics that have protective spheres around their internal phase ingredients are said to be:
    a. micellized
    b. buffered
    c. distilled
    d. chelated

    _____

34. As a process, microencapsulation is desirable because it can help ingredients avoid:
    a. defatting
    b. instability
    c. rancidity
    d. distillation

    _____

35. In cosmetics, liposomes are used to transport all of the following EXCEPT:
    a. moisturizers   c. antioxidants
    b. vitamins   d. drugs   _____

36. In cosmetics, preservatives are used to inhibit the growth of which of the following?
    a. yeast   c. fungi
    b. bacteria   d. all answers   _____

37. The process of oxidation does which of the following?
    a. adjusts pH   c. forms free radicals
    b. breaks down bacteria d. all answers   _____

38. A cosmetic product that has discoloration or odor due to oxidation is said to be:
    a. gelled   c. buffered
    b. rancid   d. chelated   _____

39. To adjust the pH of a product, which of the following agents is needed?
    a. buffering   c. chelating
    b. gellant   d. rancid   _____

40. All of the following are added to products to raise pH EXCEPT:
    a. calcium carbonate   c. tartaric acid
    b. potassium   d. sodium   _____

41. Of the following thickening and gellant agents, which is a natural chemical composed largely of fatty esters and alcohol?
    a. xanthan gum   c. methyl cellulose
    b. carbomer   d. beeswax   _____

42. Colors are added to cosmetic products for which reason?
    a. help distinguish products
    b. add aesthetic appeal
    c. reflect varying wavelengths
    d. all answers   _____

43. In the U.S. Food and Drug Administration (FDA) method of listing color names, the C in "D & C" stands for:
    a. cosmetic   c. clear
    b. color   d. certified   _____

44. According to U.S. Food and Drug Administration (FDA) guidelines, all of the following are noncertified colors EXCEPT:
    a. carmine
    b. zinc oxide
    c. aluminum oxide
    d. henna
    _____

45. Which of the following is NOT an appropriate application for certified colors?
    a. foundation
    b. mascara
    c. eyeshadow
    d. lipstick
    _____

46. Because detergents separate fats and lipids from the skin's surface, as well as dirt, makeup, and debris, they are considered what type of agent?
    a. astringent
    b. buffering
    c. exfoliating
    d. defatting
    _____

47. All of the following are disadvantages of soaps EXCEPT:
    a. low pH
    b. insufficient sebum
    c. lack of intercellular lipids
    d. drying
    _____

48. Which of the following is a role of toner?
    a. tighten the skin and pores
    b. remove cleanser residue
    c. raise pH after cleansing
    d. all answers
    _____

49. An alcohol that is denatured is:
    a. unsuitable for drinking
    b. incapable of cleansing
    c. devoid of trace elements
    d. lacking chemical structure
    _____

50. Because it attracts water to toner, propylene glycol is considered a(n):
    a. antioxidant
    b. substantive
    c. humectant
    d. surfactant
    _____

51. Skin that fails to produce enough sebum is considered:
    a. hydrophilic
    b. deionized
    c. occlusive
    d. alipidic
    _____

52. An occlusive does which of the following?
    a. stimulates sebum production
    b. prevents moisture loss
    c. tightens the skin
    d. soothes the skin
    _____

53. Emollients differ from occlusives in that they:
    a. prevent water loss   c. are lighter
    b. lie on the surface of the skin   d. none of these   ____

54. Because they have granular particles that bump or scratch the
    skin's surface to remove cells, salt crystals are considered which
    type of exfoliant?
    a. biological   c. chemical
    b. mechanical   d. none of these   ____

55. In general, which form of chemical exfoliant is used for
    combination skin?
    a. gel   c. serum
    b. cream   d. all answers   ____

56. In gel form, alpha hydroxy acids (AHAs) are appropriate for all of
    the following skin types EXCEPT:
    a. acne prone   c. combination
    b. oily   d. dry   ____

57. The plant extract that is used for its skin-firming qualities is:
    a. centella asiatica   c. matricaria
    b. aloe vera   d. hamamelis   ____

58. The common antioxidant ingredient that derives from
    pomegranates is:
    a. elagic acid   c. silymarin
    b. stearyl glycyrrhetinate   d. hypericin   ____

59. The most-used absorbing ingredient in sunscreen is which of the
    following?
    a. avobenzene   c. octisalate
    b. octinoxate   d. ecamsule   ____

60. What is the most common order of ingredients on the labels of
    skin-care and cosmetic products?
    a. spreading agents, water, performance agents, thickening
       agents
    b. thickening agents, spreading agents, water, performance
       agents
    c. water, spreading agents, thickening agents, performance
       agents
    d. performance agents, spreading agents, thickening agents,
       water   ____

CHAPTER 13—BOTANICALS AND AROMATHERAPY

1. Plant extracts that have not undergone the removal of colors, odors, or other naturally occurring compounds are said to be:
   - a. refined
   - b. absolute
   - c. isolated
   - d. whole
   ____

2. Because alpha d-tocopherol is individually separated from soy and other botanicals, it is considered a(n):
   - a. olfaction
   - b. allantoin
   - c. isolate
   - d. all answers
   ____

3. Alcohol or glycerin is needed for which of the following methods of botanical extraction?
   - a. tincture
   - b. infusion
   - c. dried herb
   - d. expeller press
   ____

4. When hot water is used to release compounds from plant material, the result is a(n):
   - a. aqueous dilution
   - b. herbal infusion
   - c. holistic isolate
   - d. herbal tincture
   ____

5. Which of the following types of fixed oil are best when expeller pressed?
   - a. jojoba
   - b. grapeseed
   - c. olive
   - d. all answers
   ____

6. As it relates to expeller pressing, the acronym RBD stands for:
   - a. refined, bleached, and deodorized
   - b. rectified, bound, and distilled
   - c. refined, blanched, and destroyed
   - d. reconstituted, bleached, and distributed
   ____

7. Supercritical extractions differ from oil distillations in that they have:
   - a. harsher approaches
   - b. heavier compounds
   - c. low concentrations
   - d. all answers
   ____

8. The botanical arnica is used for all of the following purposes EXCEPT:
   - a. arthritis
   - b. bruises
   - c. regeneration
   - d. inflammation
   ____

9. Which part of comfrey is extracted for use in skin care?
   - a. stalk
   - b. flower
   - c. seed
   - d. root
   ____

10. Which of the following botanicals is available as an oil infusion and a supercritical carbon dioxide extract?
    a. marigold
    b. sea buckthorn
    c. shea butter
    d. comfrey
    ____

11. Cranberry seed oil has which of the following properties?
    a. emollient
    b. decongestant
    c. moisturizing
    d. detoxifying
    ____

12. As an art, skill, and science, the basic goal of aromatherapy is to:
    a. maintain the body's equilibrium
    b. extract a plant's essence
    c. achieve health and well-being
    d. process odors and aromas
    ____

13. The series of brain structures activated by odor, behavior, and arousal are known as the _____ system.
    a. nervous
    b. autonomic
    c. endocrine
    d. limbic
    ____

14. Which of the following properties of essential oils have been used to heal wounds and reduce scarring and stretch marks?
    a. regeneration
    b. expectorant
    c. antispasmodic
    d. antiseptic
    ____

15. Helichrysum is especially useful for:
    a. rejuvenating cells
    b. reducing inflammation
    c. breaking up mucous
    d. serving as an antispasmodic
    ____

16. When two or more parts work together, producing a result that is greater than the total effect of the parts, the result is:
    a. tincture
    b. synergy
    c. adulteration
    d. homeostasis
    ____

17. The safest and most beneficial of the essential oils are the:
    a. monoterpene hydrocarbons
    b. esters
    c. monoterpene alcohols
    d. ethers
    ____

18. Oregano has influential amounts of which of the following?
    a. aldehydes
    b. ketones
    c. esters
    d. phenols
    ____

19. Which of the following essential oil families promotes tissue and cell formation?
    a. ketones
    b. oxides
    c. esters
    d. lactones
    ____

20. As an essential oil family, phenols have which of the following properties?
    a. expectorant
    b. immune stimulant
    c. diuretic
    d. mental stimulant
    ____

21. An essential oil is considered natural when it:
    a. has never been decolorized
    b. contains no other essential oils or vegetable oils
    c. lacks any synthetic ingredients
    d. all answers
    ____

22. An essential oil that has been rectified:
    a. has desirable colors
    b. lacks unwanted compounds
    c. has synthetic additives
    d. none of these
    ____

23. As part of an essential oil kit, Cape chamomile can be used as a(n):
    a. diuretic
    b. expectorant
    c. euphoria agent
    d. skin balancer
    ____

24. All of the following are healing properties of palmarosa EXCEPT:
    a. heart palpitations
    b. throat viral illness
    c. antiseptic
    d. cell regenerative
    ____

25. Which of the following essential oils has fungicidal properties?
    a. ylang-ylang
    b. eucalyptus
    c. cedarwood
    d. niaouli
    ____

26. For the best results, an aromatherapy practitioner will use carrier oils that are:
    a. unrefined
    b. expeller pressed
    c. organic
    d. all answers
    ____

27. Which of the following carrier oils is high in oleic fatty acids and vitamin E?
    a. olive
    b. sunflower seed
    c. rose hip seed
    d. coconut
    ____

28. When working with essential oils, which of the following dilution amount ranges is used for physical conditions that require "medicinal like" therapeutic activity?
    a. 10%–50%   c. 2.5%–5%
    b. 5%–10%   d. 0.5%–1%   ____

29. Cypress, eucalyptus globules, and grapefruit are primary components of an essential oil blend used for:
    a. conditioning mature skin
    b. treating acneic skin
    c. detoxifying/treating cellulite
    d. treating scars   ____

30. The holistic health model takes which of the following influences into account?
    a. environment   c. physical
    b. emotional   d. all answers   ____

CHAPTER 14—INGREDIENTS AND PRODUCTS FOR SKIN ISSUES

1. Which of the following is a characteristic of rinseable cleanser for oily and combination skin?
   a. soaplike consistency
   b. slight foaming
   c. slight residue
   d. all answers
   _____

2. It is NOT true that rinseable cleansers for dry and combination skin are:
   a. superfatted
   b. low in emollients
   c. best for alipidic skin
   d. all answers
   _____

3. In rinseable cleanser for very oily skin, glycolic acid serves to:
   a. condition the skin
   b. stiffen the consistency
   c. coat the skin
   d. loosen surface cells
   _____

4. In rinseable medicated cleanser for acne, which of the following serves as a mechanical exfoliant?
   a. polyethylene granules
   b. benzoyl peroxide
   c. salicylic acid
   d. hexetidine
   _____

5. Milk cleansers for oily and combination skin have a pH of about:
   a. 1.0
   b. 3.0
   c. 5.0
   d. 7.0
   _____

6. Which of the following ingredients in cleansing milk for combination skin helps make the product soothing?
   a. mineral oil
   b. emulsifier
   c. plant extract
   d. petrolatum
   _____

7. In cleansing milk for sensitive skin, which of the following is a calming agent?
   a. azulene
   b. bisabolol
   c. chamomile extract
   d. all answers
   _____

8. Which of the following ingredients is considered unnecessary in cleansing milk for dry skin?
   a. soothing agents
   b. conditioners
   c. emollient oils
   d. strengthening agents
   _____

9. Which of the following products removes excess cleanser and provides a temporary tightening effect?
   a. toner
   b. clarifying lotion
   c. astringent
   d. all answers
   _____

10. Toners, clarifying lotions, and astringents have all of the following in common EXCEPT:
    a. relatively high pH
    b. residue removal
    c. temporary pore tightening
    d. cleanser removal ____

11. Toner for oily and combination skin is best described as a:
    a. clear, water-based gel
    b. milky, alcohol-based liquid
    c. clear, water-based liquid
    d. none of these ____

12. In toner for oily and combination skin, which of the following ingredients helps restore water to dehydrated skin?
    a. citric acid   c. benzoyl peroxide
    b. glycerin derivative   d. lemon extract ____

13. Toner for extremely oily skin should be applied with a:
    a. moist brush   c. dry soft cloth
    b. dry cotton pad   d. damp sponge ____

14. Which of the following ingredients in astringent for acne-prone skin provides oil-stripping action?
    a. witch hazel distillate   c. isopropyl alcohol
    b. water   d. camphor ____

15. The toner that has a very mild astringent action and does not pull on the skin is designed for which kind of skin?
    a. normal   c. extremely oily
    b. oily and combination   d. extra-dry ____

16. In toner for normal skin, which of the following ingredients serves as a humectant?
    a. cucumber extract   c. allantoin
    b. propylene glycol   d. rose water ____

17. Which of the following is NOT a softening and soothing agent in toner for extra-dry skin?
    a. chamomile   c. glycerin
    b. mallow   d. cornflower ____

18. Many day creams are available over-the-counter (OTC) because they contain:
    a. antiobiotics   c. exfoliants
    b. moisturizers   d. sunscreens ____

19. Which of the following ingredients in day sunscreen protection fluid for oily and combination skin is a water-loss shielding agent?
   a. sodium PCA
   b. dimethicone
   c. octinoxate
   d. tocopherol ____

20. In day cream for dry and dehydrated skin, the ingredient that offers soothing properties is:
   a. octisalate
   b. aloe
   c. azulene
   d. beeswax ____

21. In sunscreen day lotions for sensitive skin, which of the following acts as a shielding protective agent?
   a. dimethicone
   b. beeswax
   c. cholesterol
   d. glycerin ____

22. The main ingredients in night treatment for oily–combination, dehydrated skin are:
   a. emollients
   b. moisturizers
   c. conditioners
   d. humectants ____

23. In night-treatment fluid for oily–combination, dehydrated skin, sodium PCA acts as a:
   a. natural moisturizing factor
   b. comedogenic ingredient
   c. conditioning agent
   d. none of these ____

24. In night treatment oily, clogged, adult skin, salicylic acid is included to provide the properties of a(n):
   a. humectant
   b. exfoliant
   c. conditioner
   d. antibacterial ____

25. Night treatment for which of the following skin types has a light, fluffy texture?
   a. oily, clogged, adult skin
   b. dehydrated, combination dry skin
   c. mature skin lacking elasticity
   d. dry, dehydrated skin ____

26. In general, serums have grown more popular than ampoules due to their:
   a. application under night cream
   b. concentrated ingredients
   c. intensive treatment
   d. ease of use ____

27. In firming serum for mature skin that lacks elasticity, which ingredient is included to improve elasticity?
    a. hyaluronic acid
    c. peptide
    b. cornflower extract
    d. all answers
    _____

28. Green tea extract is added to alpha hydroxy treatment for dry, sun-damaged skin to:
    a. prevent water loss
    c. condition the skin
    b. soothe potential irritation
    d. lower the skin's pH
    _____

29. The active ingredient in lightening-treatment gel for hyperpigmented skin is:
    a. 2% hydroquinone
    c. 10% glycolic acid
    b. magnesium ascorbyl phosphate
    d. all answers
    _____

30. In benzoyl peroxide gel for acneic skin, the role of the benzoyl peroxide is to:
    a. spread the product
    c. moisturize the skin
    b. cap the follicle
    d. exfoliate the follicle
    _____

31. Relative to the rest of the face, the skin around the eye is:
    a. less sensitive
    c. more oil-dry
    b. thicker
    d. all answers
    _____

32. Masks for dry skin contain gelling agents for what purpose?
    a. water the skin's surface layers
    b. give the masks thicker textures
    c. plump up small lines and wrinkles
    d. none of these
    _____

33. In exfoliants, which of the following acts as an abrasive agent?
    a. polyethylene granules
    c. jojoba oil beads
    b. almond meal
    d. all answers
    _____

34. In which step of the product development cycle is a product tested by actual people?
    a. ingredient selection
    c. independent testing
    b. prototoyping
    d. marketing
    _____

35. Which of the following can be used without reservation to address the prolonged redness arising from rosacea?
    a. allantoin
    c. hydrocortisone
    b. antiobiotics
    d. all answers
    _____

CHAPTER 15—PHARMACOLOGY FOR ESTHETICIANS

1. Which of the following agencies is charged with ensuring that only safe drugs reach the marketplace?
   a. Occupational Safety and Health Administration
   b. U.S. Food and Drug Administration
   c. U.S. Drug Enforcement Agency
   d. all answers ____

2. A physician's order includes all of the following EXCEPT:
   a. required pharmacy
   b. usage directions
   c. medication quantity
   d. medication strength ____

3. What is the order of elements on a properly written prescription?
   a. symbol Rx, patient signature, physician's signature, signature
   b. patient information, signature, symbol Rx, physician's signature
   c. patient information, symbol Rx, signature, physician's signature
   d. signature, patient information, physician's signature, symbol Rx ____

4. On a prescription, the signature is the:
   a. patient signature
   b. medical results
   c. prescription watermark
   d. patient instructions ____

5. A physician might prescribe which of the following to prevent or treat herpes simplex?
   a. Actos
   b. Zovirax
   c. Zoloft
   d. Lamisil ____

6. A client who is taking tetracycline may have which of the following?
   a. diabetes
   b. depression
   c. acne
   d. hypertension ____

7. In general, Cleocin T is prescribed to clients who have:
   a. acne
   b. wrinkles
   c. cold sores
   d. peel irritation ____

8. To prevent blood clotting, a client should receive:
   a. Heparin
   b. Thorazine
   c. Ambien
   d. Coumadin ____

9. The drug category that helps reduce fever is:
   a. thrombolytics   c. antipyretics
   b. expectorants   d. antiemetics   ____

10. Which of the following over-the-counter drugs blocks histamine response?
    a. Motrin   c. glycolic acid
    b. Benadryl   d. Lopressor   ____

11. All of the following are considered part of the endocrine system EXCEPT the:
    a. hypothalamus   c. thymus gland
    b. gonads   d. adrenal glands   ____

12. Women who are breast-feeding or cannot take estrogen should take which dosage of birth control pill?
    a. monophasic   c. triphasic
    b. biphasic   d. POP   ____

13. Of the types of dosage used for birth control pills, which delivers two different progesterone doses?
    a. triphasic   c. progesterone-only
    b. biphasic   d. monophasic   ____

14. Which of the following drug families limits spasms and cramping, particularly of the digestive and urinary tracts?
    a. anticoagulants   c. anticholinergics
    b. antianginals   d. antithrombotics   ____

15. Bruising is a common skin effect of which of the following drug categories?
    a. antiplatelets   c. thrombolytics
    b. lipid-lowering agents   d. anticoagulants   ____

16. Of the types of agina, which is most likely to occur on a fairly predictable schedule?
    a. unstable   c. variant
    b. sublingual   d. stable   ____

17. Temporary restriction in normal blood flow to the heart and cardiac muscles is called:
    a. myocardial ischemia   c. hypertension
    b. anaphylaxis   d. ventricular arrhythmias   ____

18. Which of the following drugs can be used to treat angina?
    a. nitrates
    b. beta blockers
    c. calcium channel blockers
    d. all answers   ____

19. Of the drugs used to treat angina, which acts by allowing greater blood flow to the heart?
    a. nitrates
    b. beta blockers
    c. calcium channel blockers
    d. all answers   ____

20. A client who presents with erythema multiform, photosensitivity, and pruritus/urticaria most likely has taken drugs from which of the following categories?
    a. calcium channel lockers
    b. antihypertensives
    c. beta blockers
    d. antiarrhythmics   ____

21. All of the following are common symptoms of an allergic reaction EXCEPT:
    a. nausea
    b. hay fever
    c. asthma
    d. eczema   ____

22. Drugs that are effective against vomiting and nausea are called:
    a. antacids
    b. antiemetics
    c. ataxias
    d. asthenias   ____

23. Of the medications used to treat the symptoms of ulcers, which relieves the symptoms of excess gas?
    a. antacids
    b. simethicone
    c. H2 blockers
    d. all answers   ____

24. Decreased sweating is a common skin effect of which of the following?
    a. antiemetics
    b. antiulcers
    c. anticholinergics
    d. antidiarrheals   ____

25. All of the following are anxiety disorders EXCEPT:
    a. obsessive-compulsive disorder
    b. phobia
    c. generalized anxiety disorder
    d. depression   ____

26. Which of the following is NOT an anticonvulsant?
    a. barbiturates
    b. valproates
    c. antianginals
    d. benzodiazepenes   ____

27. Which of the following antidepressants affect norepinephrine, serotonin, and dopamine levels?
    a. monamine oxidase inhibitors (MAOIs)
    b. tricyclic antidepressants (TCAs)
    c. selective serotonin reuptake inhibitors (SSRIs)
    d. all answers   _____

28. The drug sertraline is an example of a(n):
    a. central nervous system stimulant
    b. antidepressant
    c. antipsychotic
    d. sedative   _____

29. The common skin effects of sedatives include all of the following EXCEPT:
    a. rashes   c. pruritis
    b. photosensitivity   d. sweating   _____

30. Clients with which type of diabetes heal poorly and are at higher risk of infection?
    a. gestational   c. Type 2
    b. Type I   d. all answers   _____

31. The body's second line of defense against bacterial infections is:
    a. lysosomes
    b. T cells
    c. lymphocytes
    d. nonspecific immune responses   _____

32. Which of the following statements about methicillin-resistant Staphhylococcus aureus (MRSA) is NOT true?
    a. MRSA presents more often in old people than young
    b. there are five MRSA strains in the world
    c. MRSA tends to cause skin or soft-tissue infection
    d. people pick up MRSA through physical contact   _____

33. The process of Gram staining is designed to do which of the following?
    a. color cell components
    b. flag a diseased cell
    c. identify a bacterium
    d. all answers   _____

34. All of the following are common skin effects of antibiotics EXCEPT:
    a. photosensitivity
    b. pruritus
    c. transient redness
    d. epidermal necrolysis

    _____

35. Which of the following statements about viruses is true?
    a. they are multicellular, nonliving organisms
    b. the skin cannot fight them effectively
    c. their only purpose is nutrition
    d. Hantaviruses behave differently in different hosts

    _____

36. Which of the following inhibitors works by interfering with a virus's ability to bond with the cellular membrane?
    a. protease
    b. non-nucleoside reverse transcriptase
    c. fusion
    d. nucleoside reverse transcriptase

    _____

37. Which of the following types of mycoses affects the internal organs?
    a. systemic
    b. opportunistic
    c. superficial
    d. subcutaneous

    _____

38. Women who are of _____ body size are at greater risk of osteoporosis.
    a. average
    b. slight
    c. large
    d. all answers

    _____

39. Rheumatoid arthritis drugs can cause hirsutism, which is defined as:
    a. inflammation of the veins
    b. ringing in the ears
    c. sensation of dizziness
    d. excessive hair growth

    _____

40. A client who presents with exfoliative dermatitis and urticaria likely took which of the following classes of pain medications?
    a. nonsteroidal anti-inflammatory agents
    b. non-narcotic analgesics
    c. narcotic analgesics
    d. muscle relaxants

    _____

Part 4: Esthetics

CHAPTER 16—ADVANCED FACIAL TECHNIQUES

1. What is the proper order of the following esthetic building blocks?
    a. cleanse, exfoliate, toner, water
    b. toner, water, exfoliation, massage
    c. cleanse, water, toner, exfoliate
    d. water, toner, exfoliation, mask   ____

2. Which of the esthetic building blocks follows extraction when it is incorporated?
    a. water   c. toner
    b. massage   d. mask   ____

3. Which of the following is NOT true of the treatment for dehydrated skin?
    a. only one massage is needed in a treatment to soften dry skin
    b. the stratum corneum of very dehydrated skin resists products
    c. hydrating ultrasonic procedures are well suited to dry skin
    d. effleurage after exfoliation facilitates ampoule penetration   ____

4. For clogged, resistive skin, the esthetician should apply the building blocks in what order?
    a. massage, cleansing, mask, exfoliation
    b. cleansing, exfoliating, extraction, mask
    c. cleansing, massage, exfoliation, mask
    d. exfoliation, massage, cleansing, extraction   ____

5. For sensitive skin, all of the following should be omitted from treatment at least initially EXCEPT:
    a. exfoliation   c. physical scrubs
    b. mechanical devices   d. extraction   ____

6. In the esthetic treatment arc, all of the following are considered stimulating steps EXCEPT:
    a. exfoliation   c. massage
    b. cleansing   d. extraction   ____

7. All of the following have a vasoconstrictive effect on the circulatory system EXCEPT:
    a. cool stones   c. cool towels
    b. Lucas spray   d. hot stones   ____

8. When using wet towels, which temperature achieves the weakest skin response?
   a. tepid
   b. refrigerator cold
   c. cold
   d. cool
   _____

9. During an initial thermotherapy treatment, extraction should be limited to how many minutes?
   a. one
   b. three
   c. five to ten
   d. eighteen to twenty
   _____

10. All of the following products are irritating to sensitive skin EXCEPT:
    a. plant extracts
    b. surfactants
    c. fragrances
    d. emulsifiers
    _____

11. Which of the following is NOT recommended for sensitive skin?
    a. cool steam
    b. cold compresses
    c. extraction
    d. all answers
    _____

12. Which of the following massage types is NOT appropriate for sensitive skin?
    a. gentle tapotement
    b. Shiatsu
    c. effleurage
    d. deep manipulation
    _____

13. After treatment for sensitive skin, clients should do which of the following?
    a. use moisturizer on red areas
    b. apply sunscreen before sunbathing
    c. place cool compresses on swelling
    d. apply makeup immediately
    _____

14. For retinoid clients, the esthetician should discontinue which of the following?
    a. fragranced hydrators
    b. exfoliation treatments
    c. alcohol-based skin-care products
    d. all answers
    _____

15. When redness and peeling occur when a client starts retinoids, the client should do which of the following?
    a. use good hydrators
    b. stop use of the medication
    c. undergo exfoliation
    d. all answers
    _____

16. In manual microdermabrasion, what is the role of the carrier base?
   a. carry the crystals
   b. enhance the technique
   c. facilitate product removal
   d. all answers   _____

17. With manual microdermabrasion, the esthetician controls the result with the amount of:
   a. crystals   c. carrier
   b. pressure   d. all answers   _____

18. In manual microdermabrasion, the direct steamer should be about _____ inches from the face.
   a. 0–12   c. 18–24
   b. 12–24   d. 24–48   _____

19. In manual microdermabrasion, the technician should work in which direction on the face?
   a. clockwise   c. counterclockwise
   b. diagonally left   d. diagonally right   _____

20. Which of the following is part of manual microdermabrasion's postprocedure?
   a. using added serum as needed
   b. applying an appropriate mask
   c. applying sun protection
   d. ensuring the client has home care   _____

21. Papaya gives rise to which of the following enzymes?
   a. trypsine   c. papain
   b. pancreatin   d. bromelain   _____

22. Which of the following statements about enzymes is true?
   a. trypsine enhances exfoliation
   b. papain and AHA can commingle
   c. pancreatin has more odor than trypsine
   d. enzymes are naturally fruit smelling   _____

23. In enzyme treatments, the role of paraffin is to:
   a. dilate the follicle openings
   b. harden and flake off dead cells
   c. activate the enzyme
   d. none of these   _____

24. A client with which of the following should NOT have enzyme peeling?
    a. multiple milia
    b. dull, lifeless skin
    c. oily, clogged skin
    d. severe acne breakouts _____

25. Enzyme peels are beneficial in that they:
    a. remove the need for facials
    b. slightly constrict the pores
    c. facilitate impaction extractions
    d. all answers _____

26. Alpha hydroxy acids (AHAs) work by which of the following?
    a. adding proteins to cellular gaps
    b. loosening the "glue" of lipids
    c. sloughing off dead cells
    d. dilating follicular openings _____

27. The Cosmetic Ingredient Review of the Cosmetics, Toiletries, and Fragrance Association recommends that estheticians use alpha hydroxy acid (AHA) salon exfoliation products that have a pH of:
    a. 0
    b. 1.0
    c. 2.0
    d. 3.0 or higher _____

28. An alpha hydroxy acid (AHA) treatment should start with the:
    a. forehead
    b. chin
    c. temples
    d. nose _____

29. Beta hydroxy acid (BHA) treatments differ from alpha hydroxy acid (AHA) treatments in:
    a. setup
    b. supplies
    c. lighting source
    d. treatment area _____

30. For two weeks before administering _____ alpha hydroxy acid (AHA) treatment, the esthetician should ensure that the skin has been pretreated with lower-strength AHA.
    a. 10%
    b. 20%
    c. 30%
    d. 50% _____

31. After waxing, the esthetician should wait how long before performing an alpha hydroxy acid (AHA) treatment?
    a. six hours
    b. twenty-four hours
    c. three days
    d. seven days _____

32. Clients who have hyperpigmented skin use products like hydroquinone before alpha hydroxy acid (AHA) treatment to:
    a. identify reddened, problem areas
    b. exfoliate the dead-cell layer
    c. provide sun protection
    d. suppress melanin production   _____

33. Which of the following statements about superficial peels is true?
    a. some chemical formulas for them contain phenol
    b. they are the mildest chemical peels
    c. chemical peels are most effective with deep wrinkles
    d. all answers   _____

34. For clients with sun-damaged or hyperpigmented skin, which of the following is an alternative to clinic deep exfoliation?
    a. hydroquinone solution   c. AHA and hydroquinone
    b. low-strength AHA peel   d. all answers   _____

35. Which of the following is a potential disadvantage of deep chemical exfoliation?
    a. permanant discoloration   c. hypopigmentation
    b. allergic reaction   d. product dependence   _____

36. Superficial exfoliation will NOT do which of the following?
    a. improve fine lines and texture
    b. even the skin's coloring
    c. give a lift to the skin
    d. help lighten hyperpigmentation   _____

37. The burning sensation that sometimes accompanies liquid exfoliation lasts for about how long?
    a. 15 minutes   c. 1 hour
    b. 30 minutes   d. 3 hours   _____

38. The liquid in liquid exfoliation should be applied with which type of movement?
    a. long, horizontal   c. deep, diagonal
    b. small, circular   d. none of these   _____

39. In Jessner's treatments, frost and residue remain on the skin for about how long?
    a. fifteen minutes   c. two hours
    b. forty-five minutes   d. six hours   _____

40. After a Jessner's treatment, a client's skin may be sensitive or flushed for about how long?
   a. 10–15 minutes
   b. 15–30 minutes
   c. 12–14 hours
   d. 1–2 days
   ____

41. While the face is peeling after a cream peel, the client should NOT apply which of the following?
   a. cleanser
   b. cool water
   c. moisturizer
   d. all answers
   ____

42. After a cream peel, which of the following should be discontinued for at least two weeks?
   a. glycolic acid
   b. Retin-A
   c. sulfur
   d. all answers
   ____

43. Which of the following is a benefit of mask use?
   a. increased nutrient flow
   b. hydration
   c. purging
   d. all answers
   ____

44. An esthetician who wishes to trigger increased circulation to a client's face should apply which type of mask?
   a. purification
   b. suffocation
   c. nourishing
   d. exfoliating
   ____

45. A calming mask does which of the following?
   a. moisturizes
   b. soothes
   c. purges
   d. smoothes
   ____

46. Mint, camphor, and clove are considered rubifactants because they:
   a. rub away waste
   b. draw out moisture
   c. enhance blood flow
   d. replace dead cells
   ____

47. Which of the following might be found in a hydrating mask?
   a. ceramide
   b. comfrey
   c. caviar
   d. chamomile
   ____

48. To intensify the activity of a mask, an esthetician can do which of the following?
   a. heat with a hair dryer
   b. apply an outer layer of serum
   c. wet with warm water
   d. cover it with a cool towel
   ____

49. Collagen sheet masks are beneficial for all of the following EXCEPT:
   a. hydration
   b. oxygenation
   c. soothing
   d. rejuvenation   ____

50. Which of the following statements about specialty masks is NOT true?
   a. they usually have a serum layer
   b. sun-damaged skin responds well to them
   c. they are simpler and faster to use
   d. the first layer of a specialty mask must "set up"   ____

CHAPTER 17—ADVANCED SKIN CARE MASSAGE

1. "Around we go" is a massage technique for the:
   a. neck   c. torso
   b. arm   d. face   _____

2. Which of the following massage movements uses the palm and surface of the fingers?
   a. paddle wheel   c. around we go
   b. eye express   d. center point   _____

3. The starting point for the "center point" massage movement is the:
   a. hairline above the temples
   b. center of the forehead
   c. area between the eyebrows
   d. clavicle just below the chin   _____

4. In the "feather off" massage movement, the target treatment area is the:
   a. forehead   c. nose
   b. chin   d. eye   _____

5. All of the following are eye and face massage movements EXCEPT:
   a. paddle wheel   c. feather off
   b. center point   d. rolling along   _____

6. Which of the following is an advanced neck and décolleté movement?
   a. swim back up   c. around we go
   b. feels good   d. paddle wheel   _____

7. Which of the following advanced neck and décolleté movements uses fists?
   a. feels good   c. décolleté sweep
   b. rolling along   d. ski jump   _____

8. The first step of the "rock-a-bye" movement is to:
   a. arrange fists on the outside point of a shoulder
   b. lay palms on the outside back of a shoulder
   c. place the heels of the hands on the shoulders
   d. position the left hand on the right shoulder   _____

9. Of the following advanced back-massage movements, which starts at the waist?
   a. back sweep   c. swim back up
   b. spine munch   d. all answers   _____

10. The "spine munch" movement uses which of the following?
    a. thumb and middle or index finger
    b. pads and joints of the fingers
    c. palms and heels of the hands
    d. none of these   ____

11. Relative to acupuncture, Shiatsu is:
    a. more established   c. riskier to use
    b. easier to learn   d. all answers   ____

12. According to Shiatsu philosophy, lines and wrinkles appear on the head because the head:
    a. harbors all acupuncture points   c. carries a lot of energy
    b. stops the flow of energy   d. all answers   ____

13. An unskilled Shiatsu practitioner does which of the following?
    a. exerts pressure that comes from the body
    b. remains attuned to the client's needs
    c. feels when massage benefits the client
    d. applies pressure using the fingertips   ____

14. In Shiatsu, each point that is not particularly fatigued should be pressed how many times?
    a. one to two   c. seven
    b. three to five   d. ten   ____

15. At which point in a facial treatment should Shiatsu be performed?
    a. end   c. middle
    b. start   d. none of these   ____

16. In Shiatsu massage for the head and neck, which of the following elements are in proper order?
    a. down river, top of mountain, three-step wrinkle erase, bright eyes
    b. running water, rinse away, down river, top of mountain
    c. running water, top of mountain, bright eyes, mouth wash
    d. rinse away, down river, bright eyes, midface flush   ____

17. In Shiatsu massage for the head and neck, which of the following movements moves the thumbs to the lower edges of the nostrils?
    a. bright eyes   c. mouth wash
    b. rinse away   d. down river   ____

18. In which of the following practices do practitioners massage certain areas of the body to effect beneficial change in other areas?
   a. acupuncture
   b. homeostasis
   c. Shiatsu
   d. reflexology   _____

19. In ear reflexology massage, the last element to be performed is the:
   a. ear tug
   b. flap pinch
   c. ear roll
   d. ear pinch-roll-tug   _____

20. The use of heat and cold to trigger circulatory responses is called:
   a. thermotherapy
   b. conduction
   c. sedimentation
   d. none of these   _____

21. The type of stone that is preferred for cold stone therapy is:
   a. igneous conduction
   b. basalt composition
   c. marine sedimentary
   d. all answers   _____

22. To clear a stone's energy, an esthetician should do which of the following?
   a. process with a high-level disinfectant
   b. wash with an antibacterial soap
   c. place in a heating unit
   d. rinse in water with sea salt   _____

23. When performing stone massage for the face, all movements should be:
   a. skipping
   b. pressing
   c. gliding
   d. rolling   _____

24. Lymph drains to the preauticular nodes and the deep nodes on the neck below the earlobe from all of the following areas EXCEPT:
   a. temple
   b. nose
   c. cheeks
   d. forehead   _____

25. The conventional order of node drainage is:
   a. neck, face, scalp, inner triangle, neck
   b. face, neck, scalp, neck inner triangle
   c. face, inner triangle, neck, scalp, face
   d. inner triangle, neck, face, neck, scalp   _____

26. When starting manual lymphatic massage, it should take the esthetician about how many minutes to massage the supraclavicular nodes?
    a. twenty
    b. twelve
    c. seven
    d. three _____

27. When massaging the first section of the face in manual lymphatic massage, the first two treatment regions are the:
    a. jawline and lip
    b. chin and upper lip
    c. chin and jawline
    d. lip and mouth _____

28. When massaging the second area of the face in manual lymphatic drainage, the last area of treatment is the:
    a. posterior clavicle chain
    b. medial ends of the clavicle
    c. angle of the jaw
    d. preauricular nodes _____

29. Pressotherapy equipment is designed to:
    a. increase venous flow
    b. reduce extracellular fluid
    c. limit lymphatic flow
    d. all answers _____

30. Pressotherapy has all of the following benefits EXCEPT:
    a. improved circulation
    b. enhanced oxygen flow
    c. increased lymphatic drainage
    d. greater edema _____

CHAPTER 18—ADVANCED FACIAL DEVICES

1. The party that determines whether procedures are within the esthetician's scope of practice is the:
   a. state licensing board
   b. employer
   c. esthetician
   d. product manufacturer _____

2. An esthetician who asks questions like, "What is our business plan?" and "What services will we offer?" is doing which of the following?
   a. outlining the scope of practice
   b. analyzing the practice's needs
   c. identifying equipment options
   d. establishing company stability _____

3. When choosing which piece of equipment to buy, the esthetician should consider:
   a. training and support
   b. upgrade capabilities
   c. accessories
   d. all answers _____

4. In general, equipment leases offer all the following benefits EXCEPT:
   a. rapid approval times
   b. tax-deductible payments
   c. long-term stability
   d. low monthly fees _____

5. All of the following are reliable sources for verifying a company's stability EXCEPT:
   a. company itself
   b. Better Business Bureau
   c. other estheticians
   d. legal staff _____

6. Ideally, service contracts on esthetics equipment includes which of the following?
   a. accessory parts
   b. full labor
   c. annual preventative maintenance check
   d. all answers _____

7. Devices in which class are considered safe for all intents and purposes?
   a. I
   b. II
   c. III
   d. IV _____

8. The abnormal display of facial hyperpigmentation due to solar damage is known as:
   a. telangiectasias
   b. actinic keratosis
   c. body dysmorphia
   d. dyschromia _____

9. The most critical step in treating clients for facial rejuvenation is the technician's:
   a. education level
   b. type of device
   c. consultation ability
   d. IPL experience
   _____

10. During the consultation for facial rejuvenation, the esthetician is responsible for doing all of the following EXCEPT:
    a. serving as the treating physician
    b. providing adequate information
    c. assessing candidates' appropriateness
    d. educating clients on the procedure
    _____

11. During a consultation for facial rejuvenation, all of the following are evaluated EXCEPT:
    a. client's expectations
    b. equipment suitability
    c. tanning history
    d. facial lesions
    _____

12. Most IPL devices are cleared without reservation for use on all the following Fitzpatrick skin types EXCEPT:
    a. I
    b. III
    c. IV
    d. V
    _____

13. Clients with body dysmorphic disorder raise red flags during consultations for facial rejuvenation because they:
    a. fixate inappropriately on their bodies
    b. pose added skin-related challenges
    c. cannot respond as desired
    d. all answers
    _____

14. As they relate to facial rejuvenation, all of the following medications can be photosensitizing EXCEPT:
    a. tetracycline
    b. ibuprofen
    c. doxycycline
    d. minocycline
    _____

15. Clients who fail to follow instructions for avoiding sun exposure before and after facial rejuvenation risk which of the following?
    a. scarring
    b. hypopigmentation
    c. blisters
    d. all answers
    _____

16. A client who presents with which of the following is suitable to undergo facial rejuvenation?
    a. four months of Accutane use
    b. depression
    c. six-week-old tan
    d. lupus
    _____

17. Staff or operator eyewear for IPL photorejuvenation treatment should have an optical density of:
   a. 1
   b. 2
   c. 3
   d. 5
   _____

18. According to the protocol for IPL photorejuvenation treatment, machine calibration is conducted _____ the procedure.
   a. before
   b. during
   c. after
   d. none of these
   _____

19. The process that uses energy-producing packets of light to enhance fibroblast collagen synthesis and produce collagen is called:
   a. photomodulation
   b. photorejuvenation
   c. photodamage
   d. all answers
   _____

20. In general, light-emitting diode (LED) services are scheduled how frequently?
   a. once monthly
   b. once annually
   c. two to three times a week
   d. four to six times a year
   _____

21. Light-emitting diode (LED) treatment is used to treat all of the following EXCEPT:
   a. sunburns
   b. unidentified skin lesions
   c. stretch marks
   d. mild to moderate acne
   _____

22. Ideally, light-emitting diode (LED) treatment ends with which of the following?
   a. serum application
   b. gentle exfoliation
   c. sun protection
   d. lymphatic drainage
   _____

23. Following light-emitting diode (LED) skin treatment, which of the following is a normal response?
   a. swelling
   b. sunburn sensation
   c. rash
   d. all answers
   _____

24. For how long after photodynamic therapy (PDT) should clients avoid daylight?
   a. six hours
   b. one day
   c. two days
   d. one week
   _____

25. The process of physically exfoliating the skin is known as:
   a. microdermabrasion
   b. dyschromia
   c. electrodesiccation
   d. dysmorphia
   _____

26. Relative to esthetic microdermabrasion devices, physician microdermabrasion devices have:
    a. stronger vacuums
    b. less penetration
    c. more crystals
    d. none of these _____

27. A client who presents with which of the following should NOT be allowed to undergo microdermbrasion?
    a. sallow skin tone
    b. medium rhytids
    c. seborrhea keratosis
    d. yeast infection _____

28. In microdermabrasion, three passes are generally appropriate for what type of skin?
    a. combination
    b. normal to oily
    c. thin, dry
    d. all answers _____

29. In microdermabrasion, eye strokes with crystal devices should be from the:
    a. lower lid upward
    b. upper lid around
    c. inner corner out
    d. outer corner in _____

30. When stroking during microdermabrasion, which of the following is recommended orientation or procedure?
    a. palm downward with skin slack
    b. point of shoulder in toward décoletté
    c. forearm flexed with horizontal strokes
    d. neck hyperextended with vertical strokes _____

31. About how many microdermabrasion treatments are recommended for optimal results?
    a. four to eight
    b. eight to twelve
    c. one to two
    d. two to four _____

32. According to some manufacturers, ultrasonic technology can reduce the stratum corneum up to _____ in just one treatment.
    a. 15%
    b. 35%
    c. 75%
    d. 95% _____

33. When using ultrasonic technology, one-megahertz frequency is suitable for physical therapists treating muscle trauma because it:
    a. cools superficial tissue
    b. uses electrical current
    c. penetrates deeper
    d. all answers _____

34. In part three of an ultrasonic facial, microamp, the esthetician should hold the blade tip:
   a. downward
   b. upward
   c. flat to the skin
   d. at a 90° angle ____

35. In most states, estheticians are not allowed to perform any procedures that _____ skin tissue.
   a. cut
   b. vaporize
   c. remove
   d. all answers ____

36. In electrodesiccation treatment for skin tags, topical anesthesia should be applied how long before the procedure?
   a. 30–60 minutes
   b. 15 minutes
   c. 1–2 hours
   d. 3 hours ____

37. A current of 0.001 ampere or less is called a:
   a. nanoampere
   b. superampere
   c. cytoampere
   d. microampere ____

38. Which of the following is a benefit of microcurrent treatment?
   a. enhanced submentle chin laxity
   b. tightened jawline
   c. increased facial laxity
   d. lowered brows ____

39. To reduce marionette lines using microcurrent, the esthetician would target which of the following muscles?
   a. frontalis
   b. orbicularis oculi
   c. zygomaticus major
   d. corrugator ____

40. Steroids or antibiotics may be prescribed for which of the following complications of treatment?
   a. blistering
   b. scarring
   c. hyperpigmentation
   d. hypopigmentation ____

CHAPTER 19—HAIR REMOVAL

1. What is the most common sexually transmitted disease?
   a. HIV
   b. chlamydia
   c. genital warts
   d. pubic lice (crabs)
   ____

2. There are _____ types of HPV.
   a. over 100
   b. approximately 80
   c. fewer than 20
   d. 7
   ____

3. What is the most common area for threading?
   a. the arms
   b. the bikini area
   c. the legs
   d. the face
   ____

4. How long should the thread be for a threading procedure?
   a. 2–6 inches
   b. 8–14 inches
   c. 14–20 inches
   d. 24–30 inches
   ____

5. Sugaring is a form of hair removal that:
   a. has been used for centuries in the Middle East
   b. has been used since the 1960s in most parts of the world
   c. requires the use of a special synthetic sugar
   d. greatly irritates the skin
   ____

6. The sugar paste used in sugaring _____ after the service.
   a. inhibits bacterial growth
   b. helps reduce irritation
   c. reduces possible breakouts
   d. all answers
   ____

7. What is the minimum hair length for previously untreated hair when using the hand-applied method of sugaring?
   a. 1/16 inch
   b. 1/32 inch
   c. 1/4 inch
   d. 1/2 inch
   ____

8. Which of these is NOT a downside of using the hand-applied method of sugaring?
   a. risk of burning
   b. slow and time-consuming to perform
   c. not recommended for larger body areas such as the legs and back
   d. folliculitis and ingrown hairs may result
   ____

9. How is sugar paste made?
   a. mix sugar with a small amount of water and stir it until it takes on a pastelike consistency
   b. heat the sugar until it forms a syrup
   c. mix the sugar with an equal amount of wax, and then heat the combination in a wax heater
   d. spread paraffin wax into a sheet, sprinkle sugar and a little water onto it, and then mold it into a ball _____

10. When performing a patch test for sugaring, how long after the test should a typical histamine reaction appear?
    a. almost immediately
    b. about 1 hour
    c. within 12 hours
    d. within 48 hours _____

11. When preparing the client's skin for hand sugaring, you should NOT:
    a. treat the area with an antibacterial cleanser
    b. apply a cool compress to create goose bumps on the treatment area
    c. lightly dust the skin with a fine-grained powder
    d. lightly dust the skin with a powder free of chemicals, perfumes, and aluminum _____

12. Which of these should you use to clean the client's skin after a sugaring treatment?
    a. cotton balls or a cotton round soaked in antiseptic
    b. a spatula, which you use to scrape the residue away
    c. a warm, wet cloth
    d. a warm muslin strip _____

13. What is the primary benefit of using hard wax for hair removal?
    a. far less expensive than soft wax
    b. does not adhere to the skin
    c. requires neither preparation nor clean-up
    d. all answers _____

14. To what temperature should the wax be heated for a hard wax application?
    a. 50–70°F
    b. 75–100°F
    c. 125–160°F
    d. 175–200°F _____

15. Soft wax is more appropriate for larger body areas such as the legs and back because:
    a. using soft wax eliminates the possibility of skin sensitivity
    b. the coarseness of back and leg hair prevents it from adhering to hard wax

c. the hair can be removed quickly
d. the soft wax method is completely painless _____

16. Hard wax may break during the removal process if:
   a. the wax is too old
   b. the wax gets too cold during application
   c. the wax is applied too thinly
   d. all answers _____

17. If the client has ingrown hairs, the technician can ask the client to:
   a. release as many ingrown hairs as possible at least four days before the waxing service
   b. remove as many ingrown hairs as possible at least four days before the waxing service
   c. shave the area the day before the waxing service
   d. squeeze the area around the ingrown hair until it starts to release blood and clear fluid _____

18. Which of these is generally NOT a factor when determining the best way to shape a client's eyebrows?
   a. her age
   b. whether she wears makeup on a daily basis
   c. her ethnicity
   d. the length of her hair _____

19. If the client has a round face with wide-set eyes, you should:
   a. place the point of the arch to the outside of the iris as the client looks straight ahead
   b. bring the point of the arch to the inside of the iris as the client looks straight ahead
   c. try to eliminate the appearance of the arch altogether
   d. thin the eyebrow as much as possible to draw attention away from the eyes _____

20. When positioning the stick to determine the correct point of arch for the client's eyebrows, you should place the bottom end:
   a. at the base of the nose
   b. along the side of the nose, just above the nostril
   c. along the side of the nose, midway between the top and bottom of the nostril
   d. on the tip of the nose _____

21. When shaping the eyebrow, it should _____ from the start to the point of arch.
   a. sharply descend   c. sharply ascend
   b. gradually descend   d. gradually ascend _____

22. When speed waxing the legs, how many times should you firmly rub the strip?
    a. eight to ten
    b. five to seven
    c. one to two
    d. three to five

    _____

23. When waxing the hair of the upper arm, the wax should be applied:
    a. initially against the direction of growth, and then immediately in the direction of growth
    b. initially in the direction of growth, and then against the direction of growth
    c. only against the direction of growth
    d. only in the direction of growth

    _____

24. When blending, you:
    a. remove all of the hairs above the elbow, long and short, by applying wax and removing it with a strip
    b. remove some of the longer, more obvious hairs above the elbow, using a strip that already has wax on it
    c. leave all of the hair above the elbow intact after waxing all of the hair below the elbow
    d. apply thin beads of wax up the arm, past the elbow, and then use the strip method to remove it

    _____

25. The hair growth on the hand is usually:
    a. upward, toward the back of the hand, and angling in, toward the thumb
    b. upward, toward the back of the hand, and angling out, toward the little finger
    c. downward, toward the fingers, and angling in, toward the thumb
    d. downward, toward the fingers, and angling out, toward the little finger

    _____

26. Which of these is NOT one of the three classifications of bikini waxing?
    a. American
    b. French
    c. Japanese
    d. Brazilian

    _____

27. In a standard bikini wax, where do you remove hair?
    a. above the top of the thighs and just under the navel
    b. everywhere, including the labia and anus
    c. everywhere but a small strip on the pubis
    d. along the inner thighs

    _____

28. Which of these methods is preferred for removing hair on the labia?
    a. soft wax
    b. neither of these
    c. hard wax
    d. a combination of soft and hard wax _____

29. When removing hair from the labia, you pull:
    a. downward
    b. upward
    c. toward the inside of the leg
    d. toward the outside of the leg _____

30. How long should a client wait between Brazilian waxes if she has this service done on a regular basis?
    a. two to three weeks   c. three to four months
    b. no more than one month   d. four to six weeks _____

31. Which of these is NOT an area male clients commonly choose to have waxed?
    a. back   c. the inner ear
    b. shoulders   d. between the eyebrows _____

32. When shaping men's eyebrows, you should generally:
    a. remove the hair at the top of the nose
    b. try to create high arches
    c. aim for a sophisticated look
    d. refrain from any type of tweezing _____

33. When waxing a man's back, where should you begin?
    a. the area just below the shoulders
    b. the area just above the waistband of the pants
    c. in the center of the back
    d. on the hairiest area of the back _____

34. If the client develops hives on the back after waxing:
    a. you should contact a doctor
    b. you should apply hydrocortisone cream
    c. they will subside in about an hour
    d. they will subside in a day or two _____

35. When waxing a man's chest, the hair must be:
    a. no more than 1/4 inch long
    b. at least 1 inch long
    c. at least 3/4 inch long
    d. approximately 1/2 inch long _____

36. Hair removal with intense pulsed light (IPL) is appropriate for which skin type?
    a. Type I
    b. Type III
    c. Type V
    d. all answers

37. Compared to other treatment modalities, laser hair removal:
    a. presents some risk of disease transmission via blood
    b. can treat large body areas fasters
    c. produces temporary results
    d. is more uncomfortable than electrolysis

38. Intense pulsed light (IPL) hair removal:
    a. presents safety concerns for the eyes
    b. is inexpensive
    c. is most effective on light and nonpigmented hair
    d. is generally effective on dark or tanned skin

39. Before performing laser hair removal, you should:
    a. remove all reflective clothing and jewelry
    b. make sure that you and the client are wearing protective eyewear
    c. be wearing a lab coat and comfortable shoes
    d. all answers

40. What is hypertrichosis?
    a. decreased nonandrogen-dependent hair growth
    b. decreased androgen-dependent hair growth
    c. increased nonandrogen-dependent hair growth
    d. increased androgen-dependent hair growth

41. A person with which of these skin types is the best candidate for laser hair removal?
    a. Type III
    b. Type I
    c. Type VI
    d. Type V

42. Which of these is NOT a contraindication for laser hair removal?
    a. open wounds
    b. diabetes
    c. sunburned skin
    d. history or keloid scarring

43. The primary objectives of the consultation are:
    a. education and determination of candidacy
    b. education and determination of affordability
    c. determination of candidacy and client referrals
    d. determination of affordability and client referrals

44. On the day of the appointment, before beginning the laser hair-removal treatment, it's important to:
    a. rub a mild, fragrance-free massage oil into the area to be treated to help prevent burning
    b. leave the treatment area unshaved
    c. tell the client to avoid tweezing and waxing
    d. verify that the client has signed a consent form ____

45. It's important to remember that if a client chooses to use a topical anesthetic before a laser hair removal procedure:
    a. the client must attain a physician's approval for the procedure
    b. the skin may temporarily turn darker
    c. the skin may temporarily turn lighter
    d. the client must obtain a doctor's prescription for the anesthetic ____

46. Which of these should NOT be used during a laser hair removal session?
    a. antiseptic lotion
    b. gloves
    c. paper towels
    d. linens ____

47. Which of these laser hair-removal procedure steps should you do FIRST?
    a. select the starting spot
    b. unlock the laser device
    c. wipe the skin down with soothing antiseptic lotion
    d. set the treatment parameters ____

48. To cool the skin before a laser hair-removal treatment, it is often suggested that you apply ice packs:
    a. for 30–45 seconds
    b. until the client feels uncomfortable
    c. for about 3 minutes
    d. for at least 5 minutes ____

49. With laser hair removal, how is spot size measured?
    a. in millimeters
    b. in centimeters
    c. in inches
    d. in decimeters ____

50. Thermal relaxation time (TRT) is the time it takes for
    _____ heat energy to be dissipated from the target tissue.
    a. 100%
    b. 25%
    c. 75%
    d. 50% ____

51. If the client undergoes Nd:YAG hair removal treatments, he or she should avoid the sun for:
    a. three to four months
    c. one to two weeks
    b. four to six days
    d. four to six weeks ____

52. After a laser hair-removal treatment, the client should be instructed to take _____ showers.
    a. long, cool
    c. quick, hot
    b. quick, warm
    d. quick, cool ____

53. If a client experiences splattering after a laser hair-removal treatment, it means:
    a. some of the client's hair was singed
    b. the client experienced some swelling
    c. the client experienced some redness of the skin
    d. the client's skin developed tiny bumps resembling goose bumps ____

54. An action or effect of a drug or treatment other than the desired effect is considered a:
    a. complication
    c. treatment consequence
    b. side effect
    d. none of these ____

55. Which of these is NOT a potential complication of laser hair removal?
    a. blistering
    c. hyperpigmentation
    b. scarring
    d. intense pruritus ____

CHAPTER 20—ADVANCED MAKEUP

1. Semipermanent lashes provide a fuller, more natural appearance because they:
   a. require added adhesives
   b. attach to existing synthetic lashes
   c. apply singly to individual lashes
   d. none of these ____

2. A client who presents with which of the following should be disallowed from receiving synthetic lashes?
   a. hair loss   c. contact lenses
   b. erythema   d. blepharitis ____

3. Should adhesive contact the skin during synthetic lash application, the esthetician should first apply:
   a. adhesive remover   c. saline
   b. water   d. none of these ____

4. The first step in emergency eye-cleansing protocol is to:
   a. open the eye as wide as possible
   b. flush with warm water
   c. flush with sterile eyewash solution
   d. seek medical attention ____

5. When applying synthetic lashes, the technician should avoid adhesives with:
   a. clear colorations   c. expiration dates
   b. strong odors   d. batch numbers ____

6. The main purpose of the eyelash and eyelid is to:
   a. lubricate the eye   c. stabilize the eye
   b. allow movement   d. provide protection ____

7. Eyelashes placed at which stage in the life cycle last the longest?
   a. catagen   c. halogen
   b. anagen   d. telogen ____

8. Eyelashes applied to create a dramatic look are how many times longer than the client's lashes?
   a. 1/8   c. 1/3
   b. 1/4   d. 1/2 ____

9. The longest-lasting synthetic lashes are classified as looking:
   a. dramatic   c. natural
   b. feminine   d. maximum ____

10. When practicing synthetic lash application on a mannequin, the first step is to apply the:
    a. gel pad
    b. lower lashes
    c. adhesive along upper lash line
    d. strip along brow bone _____

11. In the second step of semipermanent eyelash-extension application, when gel pads are placed above the upper lashes, the client's eyes should be:
    a. closed   c. half-open
    b. open   d. taped shut _____

12. Once semipermanent eyelash extensions have been applied, many manufacturers recommend coating the lashes with a moisture barrier for how long immediately following the procedure?
    a. 10 minutes   c. 12 hours
    b. 30 minutes   d. 24 hours _____

13. Once semipermanent eyelash extensions have been applied, clients should avoid getting them wet for how long immediately following the procedure?
    a. 15 minutes   c. 24 hours
    b. 30 minutes   d. 48 hours _____

14. In an eye with an almond contour, the longest extensions appear where on the eye?
    a. inner corner   c. center portion
    b. outside corner   d. all answers _____

15. Synthetic lashes are NOT available in which of the following thicknesses, measured in millimeters?
    a. 0.05   c. 0.15
    b. 0.10   d. 0.20 _____

16. Lashes commonly fall off for all the following reasons EXCEPT:
    a. excessive dryness   c. life cycle
    b. poor technique   d. mascara residue _____

17. It is accurate to say that mineral makeup serves as which of the following?
    a. sunscreen   c. foundation
    b. concealer   d. all answers _____

18. Because the minerals used in powders are inert, they:
    a. remain on the face for long periods
    b. cannot support bacterial life
    c. contain talc and colorants
    d. mix easily in solution   _____

19. Which of the following minerals gives skin-care products slip and glide?
    a. zinc oxide   c. mica
    b. boron nitride   d. iron oxide   _____

20. Dimethicone is commonly coated on titanium dioxide to increase the mineral's:
    a. oxidation elimination   c. light-scattering abilities
    b. sun protection factor   d. all answers   _____

21. Boron nitride is known as the "soft focus" mineral because it:
    a. refracts light   c. slips on the skin
    b. covers the eye   d. provides sheen   _____

22. Titanium dioxide derives from all of the following EXCEPT:
    a. anatase   c. brookite
    b. rutile   d. hematite   _____

23. All of the following are roles of bismuth oxychloride EXCEPT:
    a. colorant provider   c. covering agent
    b. sun protectant   d. adhesion agent   _____

24. Talc accounts for about _____ of mineral makeup.
    a. 0%   c. 30%–50%
    b. 10%–20%   d. 70%–90%   _____

25. Which of the following compounds is considered a sensitizer?
    a. FD&C dyes   c. synthetic fragrances
    b. preservatives   d. all answers   _____

26. Mineral makeups resist running, creasing, and smearing because they:
    a. come in liquid/powder form   c. create surface tension
    b. have uniform particle size   d. all answers   _____

27. On sunscreen, the SPF rating refers to which of the following protections?
    a. UVA only   c. both UVA and UVB
    b. UVB only   d. neither UVA nor UVB   _____

28. Powder that is slightly lighter than the skin's tone is appropriate for which of the following Fitzpatrick skin types?
    a. III
    b. I
    c. V
    d. II ____

29. When the esthetician applies mineral makeup before moisturizer has absorbed, the resulting appearance is:
    a. uneven and blotchy
    b. excessively shiny
    c. pronounced pores
    d. accentuated fine lines ____

30. When mineral makeup accentuates pores or fine lines, the esthetician should do which of the following?
    a. switch to pressed powder
    b. spritz the affected area
    c. pat on moisturizer
    d. all answers ____

31. Cosmetic camouflage is founded on the notion that the color _____ best masks redness.
    a. violet
    b. yellow
    c. green
    d. blue ____

32. Plastic surgery is most commonly done on which of the following body parts?
    a. abdomen
    b. thighs
    c. eyelids
    d. nose ____

33. A client whose skin is thinning below the eyes would likely present with undereye circles of what color?
    a. blue/purple
    b. brown to gray
    c. blue/gray
    d. purple/gray ____

34. Brown is the most difficult color to conceal because it:
    a. has multiple complementary colors
    b. resides on the dark end of the spectrum
    c. approximates the color of cosmetics
    d. represents a mixture of colors ____

35. When applying concealer, which of the following strokes best ensures that the concealer will cover the face?
    a. horizontal
    b. criss-cross
    c. upward
    d. downward ____

36. The best finger for concealer application is the:
    a. index
    b. thumb
    c. ring
    d. pinkie ____

37. Scar tissue lacks which of the following?
    a. hair follicles   c. sweat glands
    b. strong UV resistance   d. all answers   _____

38. A bruise in its final healing stages is best concealed by the color:
    a. lilac   c. yellow
    b. brown   d. green   _____

39. Relative to traditional makeup techniques, airbrushing:
    a. takes more time   c. achieves less precision
    b. uses less makeup   d. none of these   _____

40. A top-fed airbrush would be best used for which of the following?
    a. body makeup   c. beauty makeup
    b. tanning   d. all answers   _____

41. When airbrushing, spray patterns are based on which of the
    following?
    a. brush control   c. spray force
    b. cosmetic type   d. brush distance   _____

42. In cosmetics application, a dash is defined as a(n):
    a. long brush stroke   c. abbreviated treatment
    b. pause in application   d. ending element   _____

43. When applying airbrush makeup using the narrow spray pattern,
    the esthetician should hold the airbrush how many inches from
    the skin?
    a. 1 or less   c. 1/4–3
    b. 3–6   d. less than 1/4   _____

44. The slightly tacky plastic film used by airbrush artists to create
    templates is called _____ film.
    a. freeform   c. faraway
    b. frisket   d. none of these   _____

45. Of the following cosmetic procedures, which is requested most
    often?
    a. areola   c. cheek color
    b. lip color   d. eyeliner   _____

Part 5: Spas

CHAPTER 21—SPA TREATMENTS

1. All of the following are recognized spa types EXCEPT:
   a. day
   b. psychotherapy
   c. resort
   d. destination
   _____

2. Which of the following types of spa offers physical therapy, water therapy, and specialized exercise programs in addition to spa treatments?
   a. resort spa
   b. day spa
   c. wellness center
   d. hospital center
   _____

3. Naturopaths and chiropractors are most likely to be employed by which of the following types of spa?
   a. wellness center
   b. health club
   c. destination spa
   d. day spa
   _____

4. The Health Insurance Portability and Accountability Act (HIPAA) helps ensure which core tenet of the spa?
   a. sterility
   b. variety
   c. confidentiality
   d. effectiveness
   _____

5. It is acceptable for the esthetician to disclose private client information when:
   a. other staff members request the information
   b. harm may arise from failing to do so
   c. cases become very complex and time consuming
   d. all answers
   _____

6. Before performing any treatment, the esthetician should do which of the following with the client?
   a. document health history
   b. identify contraindications
   c. take a skin history
   d. all answers
   _____

7. Which of the following is a general contraindication for body treatments?
   a. acne lesions
   b. rosacea
   c. varicose veins
   d. erythema
   _____

8. On the treatment table, the outermost layer of material corresponds to the _____ treatment that is performed.
   a. first
   b. last
   c. most complex
   d. most messy
   _____

9. On the treatment table, the bottom-most layer is a:
   a. wool blanket
   b. conventional sheet
   c. large towel
   d. plastic sheet
   _____

10. When reviewing the client's health history in preparation for treatment, the esthetician should do all of the following EXCEPT:
    a. review and clarify all issues of modesty
    b. familiarize with the client's health history form
    c. raise conversational topics that are off topic
    d. avoid a clinical or medicinal approach
    _____

11. When preparing a client for treatment, which of the following steps occurs last?
    a. review client's health history
    b. provide directions for table placement
    c. discuss concerns with other staff
    d. discuss modesty issues
    _____

12. In the process of arranging the client in the treatment room, which of the following steps should occur last?
    a. drape the client's hair
    b. review the client's health history
    c. identify the draping sheet
    d. apply any modesty towels
    _____

13. The key to any successful body treatment is:
    a. relaxation
    b. preparation
    c. sterilization
    d. detachment
    _____

14. A client who relaxes regularly exhibits all of the following qualities EXCEPT:
    a. improved ability to concentrate
    b. increased energy and activity levels
    c. enhanced responsiveness to stress hormones
    d. decreased metabolic heart rate
    _____

15. Which of the following helps create a relaxing environment for the client?
    a. running water
    b. soft-soled shoes
    c. bright lighting
    d. all answers
    _____

16. Estheticians can help clients overcome modesty issues by doing which of the following?
    a. describing treatment fully
    b. explaining the draping protocol
    c. allowing private time for disrobing
    d. all answers

    _____

17. A shower immediately following treatment should be what temperature initially?
    a. cool
    b. warm
    c. tepid
    d. hot

    _____

18. A body treatment that involves applying an exfoliating, hydrating, detoxifying mask to the body is known as a(n):
    a. body wrap
    b. body mask
    c. blanket wrap
    d. elastic wrap

    _____

19. Which of the following treatments relies on the use of hot and cold?
    a. body mask
    b. body wrap
    c. blanket wrap
    d. all answers

    _____

20. Of these ingredients used in body treatments, which is commonly used in cellulite creams?
    a. camphor
    b. caffeine
    c. sulfur
    d. kaolin

    _____

21. The vitamin that sometimes help treat psoriasis is:
    a. E
    b. A
    c. C
    d. D

    _____

22. The ingredient that is most similar in structure to caffeine is:
    a. theophylline
    b. collagen
    c. sulfur
    d. elastin

    _____

23. Green tea extract contains catechins, which are:
    a. neutralizers
    b. moisturizers
    c. antioxidants
    d. all answers

    _____

24. Body wraps work on the principle of occlusion, which means that they _____ on the skin.
    a. prevent chemical reactions
    b. keep product in place
    c. attach to hair follicles
    d. none of these

    _____

25. Ingredients like clays and muds are added to body wraps to:
    a. remove dead cells
    c. decrease temperature
    b. eliminate perspiration
    d. draw out toxins
    _____

26. In seaweed wraps, ingredients like vitamins and minerals serve the purpose of:
    a. providing a pleasing fragrance
    b. exfoliating the skin's surface
    c. breaking up fatty deposits
    d. raising the skin's temperature
    _____

27. In general, a seaweed wrap is applied with which of the following?
    a. damp towel
    c. long spatula
    b. gloved hands
    d. all answers
    _____

28. What is the role of hydrocollators in herbal wraps?
    a. increase circulation
    c. heat the herbal wraps
    b. dehydrate the herbal mixture
    d. soothe the skin
    _____

29. A typical herbal wrap treatment lasts for about how long?
    a. fifteen minutes
    c. one hour
    b. thirty minutes
    d. three hours
    _____

30. Linen is the preferred material for herbal wraps because it:
    a. maintains heat
    c. stiffens quickly
    b. dissolves slowly
    d. all answers
    _____

31. After an herbal wrap, the client should do which of the following?
    a. avoid immediate showering
    c. rest as much as possible
    b. drink plenty of water
    d. all answers
    _____

32. When performing an herbal wrap, the first layer placed on the treatment bed is a:
    a. wool blanket
    c. water protective cover
    b. bath towel
    d. metallic spa sheet
    _____

33. Thalassotherapy is defined as which of the following?
    a. creation of heat for herbal wrapping
    b. process of producing or increasing perspiration
    c. removal of wastes and impurities
    d. therapeutic use of the beneficial effects of sea water
    _____

34. In an herbal scrub, almond meal serves as which kind of agent?
    a. cleansing   c. antioxidant
    b. moisturizing   d. nutritious   ____

35. An herbal scrub intended as an antioxidant should contain:
    a. vitamin E oil   c. oat powder
    b. apricot kernel oil   d. honey   ____

36. Which ingredient of an herbal wrap is effective with arthritis and sore muscles?
    a. clove   c. lavender
    b. ginger   d. allspice   ____

37. To provide toning and stimulation, an herbal wrap should have:
    a. basil   c. rosemary
    b. burdock   d. clove   ____

38. Which of the following supplies is used to break up masks for removal?
    a. spatulas   c. thermal blankets
    b. exfoliating gloves   d. all answers   ____

39. Which of the following types of wrap is designed to aid in the detoxification process?
    a. cellophane body   c. Kneipp body
    b. dry blanket   d. cool moist blanket   ____

40. All of the following are therapeutic effects of music EXCEPT:
    a. decreased stress hormones
    b. increased productivity
    c. slowed brain waves
    d. lowered endorphin levels   ____

CHAPTER 22—ALTERNATIVE THERAPIES

1. The life force energy of all living things is called:
    a. essence
    b. energy body
    c. spirit
    d. all answers
    ____

2. The energy body is fullest at which stage of life?
    a. birth
    b. early childhood
    c. adolescence
    d. adulthood
    ____

3. Which of the following contributes to the health of the physical, mental, and emotional bodies?
    a. inner face
    b. outer face
    c. both a and b
    d. neither a nor b
    ____

4. Clients are susceptible to Leaky Aura Syndrome when they:
    a. move with their auras
    b. lose pieces of their energies
    c. become full of their own energies
    d. resonate new energies
    ____

5. All of the following create free radicals EXCEPT:
    a. antioxidants
    b. processed sugar
    c. prescription drugs
    d. tobacco
    ____

6. As an energy management component, the physical body does all of the following EXCEPT:
    a. connects sensory nature to nature's rhythm
    b. links sensory intelligence and the sensory nervous system
    c. processes information from life experiences
    d. all answers
    ____

7. Which of the following rejuvenates a depleted spirit?
    a. Reiki
    b. flower essences
    c. gemstones
    d. all answers
    ____

8. The most powerful of the senses is:
    a. touch
    b. smell
    c. taste
    d. feel
    ____

9. The essential oils in plants behave similarly to which of the following in the human body?
    a. hormones
    b. blood
    c. bones
    d. muscles
    ____

10. What is the spiritual effect of the essential oil melissa?
    a. enhances mental clarity   c. lifts the spirits
    b. calms the emotions   d. none of these   ____

11. Which of the following statements about herbs is NOT true?
    a. they are taken internally
    b. they work most on the physical body
    c. they come in tea form only
    d. they balance the mental and emotional bodies   ____

12. All of the following herbs enhance memory recall EXCEPT:
    a. rosemary   c. gotu kola
    b. ginkgo biloba   d. chamomile   ____

13. In general, clients take the herb lemon balm to do which of the
    following?
    a. enhance mental clarity   c. lift the spirits
    b. calm the emotions   d. improve memory recall ____

14. The word *psychology* was derived from the word *psyche*, meaning:
    a. soul   c. behavior
    b. breath   d. emotion   ____

15. When practicing breathing exercises, it is recommended to
    breathe in _____ and breathe out _____.
    a. confidence, doubt   c. gratitude, anxiety
    b. anger, love   d. judgments, fear   ____

16. The chakras are to the spirit as the _____ are to the body.
    a. arteries   c. bones
    b. thoughts   d. organs   ____

17. People's programming and conditioning are associated with which
    of the following chakras?
    a. three   c. seven
    b. five   d. nine   ____

18. The healing and balancing energy that is transmitted through the
    palms is known as:
    a. aura   c. Reiki
    b. chakra   d. none of these   ____

19. The "ki" portion of the word *Reiki* means:
    a. energy management   c. universal energy
    b. life force energy   d. mental chatter   ____

20. Reiki exits the body through which of the following?
    a. hands   c. head
    b. heart   d. all answers   ____

21. Attunement to Reiki lasts for how long?
    a. 25 minutes   c. 10 months
    b. 24 hours   d. lifetime   ____

22. What is the recommended waiting period between Reiki attunements?
    a. three days   c. two weeks
    b. one week   d. three months   ____

23. At which level of Reiki can practitioners activate others?
    a. four   c. two
    b. three   d. one   ____

24. In a human, Dr. Edward Bach's flower essences would be like the:
    a. spirit   c. skeleton
    b. brain   d. heart   ____

25. Flower essences are applied in which of the following ways?
    a. spraying in a mist   c. placing on the pulse points
    b. ingesting them orally d. all answers ____

26. A client seeking protection from outside sources should take which of the following Bach flower essences?
    a. white chestnut c. walnut
    b. larch   d. rock water   ____

27. Vervain is the Bach flower essence believed to do which of the following?
    a. find middle ground   c. heal emotional wounds
    b. clear mental chatter d. improve self-confidence ____

28. An object, a stone, or jewelry believed to give the wearer magical powers is called a:
    a. scry   c. chakra
    b. talisman   d. complement   ____

29. Placing blue lace agate on the fifth chakra does which of the following?
    a. opens the heart to love and self-nurture
    b. inspires sensuality and receptivity
    c. enhances clarity of thought and communication
    d. provides a peaceful place for stress release ____

30. Which of the following is NOT a question asked before and after a rejuvenation procedure to provide benchmarks for treatment?
    a. How would you rate your stress level?
    b. Have you ever had this type of treatment before?
    c. At what level is your mental chatter?
    d. Where would you place your emotional/anxiety level? ___

CHAPTER 23—AYURVEDA THEORY AND TREATMENTS

1. Ayurveda is the science or study of:
   a. longevity
   b. actions
   c. meditation
   d. digestion
   _____

2. In the six-sense approach defined in the first vedic principle, the sheets, robes, and blankets of the esthetician's treatment room all factor into:
   a. smell
   b. sight
   c. heart feeling
   d. touch
   _____

3. The esthetician who is interested in clients' work and home lives, how well they sleep, and what makes them tick most closely models which vedic principle?
   a. one
   b. two
   c. three
   d. five
   _____

4. All of the following are panchamahabhutas EXCEPT:
   a. space
   b. earth
   c. love
   d. fire
   _____

5. An invisible force that is responsible for all physiological and psychological processes in the body/mind system is called a(n):
   a. ama
   b. mala
   c. guna
   d. dosha
   _____

6. Which of the three doshas combine the qualities of space, air, water, fire, and earth?
   a. pitta
   b. kapha
   c. vatta
   d. all answers
   _____

7. Which of the following doshas is responsible for voluntary and involuntary body movement?
   a. vata
   b. nadi
   c. kapha
   d. pitta
   _____

8. Earth and water qualities combine in the dosha known as:
   a. vata
   b. kapha
   c. pitta
   d. none of these
   _____

9. Prakruti is which of the following?
   a. psychic power
   b. combination of doshas
   c. state of pure joy
   d. imbalance of doshas
   _____

10. The air element comes in which of the two following states?
    a. cool and upward moving
    b. cold and heat
    c. active and inspiration
    d. active and open   ____

11. All of the following elements undergo constant change EXCEPT:
    a. air   c. space
    b. fire   d. water   ____

12. A client who presents with dry, flaky skin is assumed to have an excess of which of the following elements?
    a. fire   c. water
    b. space   d. air   ____

13. A client who presents with a small, slender build and light musculature most likely has which type of body?
    a. vata   c. kapha
    b. pitta   d. none of these   ____

14. All of the following are key words for balancing the vata dosha EXCEPT:
    a. relax   c. warm
    b. nourish   d. calm   ____

15. All of the following would be appropriate snacks for the vata client EXCEPT:
    a. brownies   c. iced tea
    b. cookies   d. crackers   ____

16. When treating a client whose vata is high, the esthetician should do all of the following EXCEPT:
    a. engage in as little conversation possible
    b. maintain a warm room temperature
    c. encourage the client to sleep
    d. apply a firm, strong touch   ____

17. A typical pitta client is which of the following?
    a. fine boned   c. powerful
    b. square   d. self-conscious   ____

18. Which of the following can trigger an imbalance in pitta dosha?
    a. comfort foods
    b. overexercising
    c. spicy foods
    d. none of these answers   ____

122

19. Pitta dosha is prone to increasing under which of the following conditions?
    a. outside exercise
    b. tight schedule
    c. calm state
    d. cool weather
    _____

20. All of the following are key words in pitta dosha treatment EXCEPT:
    a. freshen
    b. relax
    c. cool
    d. soothe
    _____

21. Which of the following dosha types tend to be most challenging?
    a. pitta
    b. vata
    c. kapha
    d. agni
    _____

22. Which of the following techniques are recommended for pitta dosha clients?
    a. cool compresses
    b. seaweed wraps
    c. mud masks
    d. all answers
    _____

23. A kapha dosha client should be offered all of the following snacks EXCEPT:
    a. apple juice
    b. saltine crackers
    c. pineapple wedges
    d. carrot slices
    _____

24. Which of the following describes a typical kapha client?
    a. slightly built
    b. insecure
    c. somber
    d. soft spoken
    _____

25. The key word for treatment that balances the kapha dosha is:
    a. comfort
    b. freshen
    c. stimulate
    d. all answers
    _____

26. When treating a client with a kapha imbalance, the esthetician should do all of the following EXCEPT:
    a. serve spicy snacks
    b. stroke deeply
    c. use very warm water
    d. inspire conversation
    _____

27. Which of the following snacks should the esthetician serve the kapha dosha client?
    a. pretzels
    b. salsa
    c. plain rolls
    d. green peppers
    _____

28. The kaph dosha client who is seeking balance should do which of the following?
    a. eat many vegetables
    b. have heavy breakfasts
    c. maximize water intake
    d. consume cold foods
    _____

29. In ayurvedic theory, which of the following types of beauty is in the middle of the scale?
    a. outer
    b. inner
    c. secret
    d. none of these

    ____

30. Applied topically, essential oils are _____ more medicinally powerful than ingested herbs.
    a. 5%–10%
    b. 20%–30%
    c. 45%–50%
    d. 60%–75%

    ____

31. Which of the following is an ingredient in ayurvedic skin care?
    a. ground almonds
    b. tumeric
    c. citrus peel
    d. sugar

    ____

32. Which of the following herbs is believed to be mentally nurturing and clarifying?
    a. ashwaganda
    b. shatavari
    c. manjistha
    d. rudraksha

    ____

33. All of the following are properties of the herb neem EXCEPT:
    a. moisturizer
    b. blood detoxifer
    c. skin toner
    d. astringent

    ____

34. Which of the following blends should be warming, luxurious, and comforting?
    a. pitta
    b. kapha
    c. aura
    d. vata

    ____

35. Lavender, nutmeg, and orange are essential oils typically found in a _____ blend.
    a. vata
    b. pitta
    c. yantra
    d. kapha

    ____

36. Vital, hidden, or secret energy points on the body are known as:
    a. marmas
    b. ashrams
    c. samadis
    d. gunas

    ____

37. The esthetician would massage which of the following marma points to ease eye strain and headaches?
    a. kopola nasa
    b. ashru antara
    c. shankha
    d. oshta

    ____

38. In a basic marma point massage, which of the following marma points are in correct order?
    a. karnamula, krikatika, mantha
    b. mantha, simanta, akshaka
    c. shivarandra, karnamula, krikatika
    d. none of these   ____

39. In an opening sequence massage, which of the following is treated immediately after the calf muscle?
    a. knees   c. shoulders
    b. neck   d. ankles   ____

40. Aryuvedic mud is applied for which of the following reasons?
    a. eased eye tension
    b. enhanced blood flow
    c. cleansing and rejuvenation
    d. all answers   ____

Part 6: Medical

CHAPTER 24—WORKING IN A MEDICAL SETTING

1. The role of the esthetician has expanded in modern day to include which of the following?
   a. personal counseling
   b. all-inclusive skin care
   c. scientific research
   d. medical training
   _____

2. As technology has expanded, the esthetician's status as a medical professional has:
   a. expanded
   b. declined
   c. not changed
   d. disappeared
   _____

3. Which of the following are noninvasive procedures?
   a. collagen
   b. Botox® injections
   c. microdermabrasion
   d. all answers
   _____

4. Baby boomers are among the most significant contributors to esthetics innovations because they:
   a. have large disposable incomes
   b. desire results-oriented treatments
   c. wish to retain a youthful appearance
   d. all answers
   _____

5. The scope of practice does which of the following?
   a. prioritizes all of the esthetician's work tasks
   b. assigns levels of proficiency to professional estheticians
   c. determines which treatments the esthetician can provide
   d. none of these
   _____

6. The role of each state's Board of Registration for Estheticians is to:
   a. provide legal counsel on services
   b. define regulations for scopes of practice
   c. align nursing regulations with esthetics regulations
   d. regulate licensing for medical personnel
   _____

7. Which of the following medical specialties is NOT commonly associated with medical aesthetics?
   a. hematology
   b. dermatology
   c. plastic surgery
   d. cosmetic surgery
   _____

8. A holistic approach to health, beauty, and wellness is being fueled by which of the following?
   a. continuing success of managed care
   b. industry financial opportunity
   c. limitations of technology
   d. all answers ____

9. Dermatologists are medical professionals who:
   a. study the body system producing hormones
   b. specialize in conditions of the foot
   c. coordinate the care of cancer patients
   d. specialize in diseases of the skin, hair, and nails ____

10. All of the following are considered appearance-related skin conditions EXCEPT:
    a. hyperpigmentation   c. skin cancer
    b. hyperplasia   d. wrinkles ____

11. Advanced dermatological procedures like laser skin resurfacing fall into the realm of the _____ surgeon.
    a. dermatological   c. reconstructive
    b. cosmetic plastic   d. all answers ____

12. All of the following fall into the realm of the cosmetic plastic surgeon EXCEPT:
    a. liposuction   c. rhytidectomy
    b. melanoma   d. blepharoplasty ____

13. College courses are based on a _____ hour system.
    a. clock   c. transfer
    b. substitute   d. credit ____

14. In the medical education model, a doctoral degree generally takes how many years to complete?
    a. one   c. four
    b. two   d. eight ____

15. As the foundation of education, the licensed nurse practitioner (LPN) completes which of the following?
    a. one-year internship
    b. two years of training
    c. four-year college curriculum
    d. two-year master's degree ____

16. The scientific method is a philosophy of reasoning based on:
    a. testing theories   c. false assumptions
    b. discounting controls   d. all answers   _____

17. In scientific research, the role of a placebo is to:
    a. support unusual evidence
    b. disprove all theories
    c. inspire new hypotheses
    d. appear like a tested substance   _____

18. In which step of the scientific method does the researcher raise a question about what has been observed?
    a. fourth   c. second
    b. third   d. first   _____

19. The factors that can affect an experiment are known as:
    a. placebos   c. characteristics
    b. variables   d. controls   _____

20. In the SOAP method of charting, the *P* stands for:
    a. plan   c. personal
    b. precision   d. perception   _____

CHAPTER 25—MEDICAL TERMINOLOGY

1. The universal language of medicine is based on the work of
   _____.
   a. Imhotep   c. Salk
   b. Hippocrates   d. Jung   ____

2. The goal of word analysis is to:
   a. identify who created a word
   b. determine a proper word substitute
   c. unlock the meaning of a word
   d. all answers   ____

3. When examining a medical word, the esthetician should examine
   its parts in what order?
   a. beginning, end, middle
   b. end, beginning, middle
   c. beginning, middle, end
   d. middle, end, beginning   ____

4. In the word *leukocyte*, what is the combining vowel?
   a. u   c. e
   b. o   d. all answers   ____

5. What is the root of the word *otolaryngologist*?
   a. ot   c. logist
   b. laryng   d. a and b   ____

6. What is the connector vowel in the word *intravenous*?
   a. ous   c. ven
   b. intra   d. none of these   ____

7. The plural form of the word *thorax* is:
   a. thoraces   c. thorases
   b. thoraxes   d. none of these   ____

8. When the word *foramen* is pluralized, the result is:
   a. foramens   c. foramina
   b. foramex   d. foramenses   ____

9. Which of the following is the plural form of the word *cornu*?
   a. cornus   c. cornia
   b. cornua   d. cornex   ____

10. Which of the following root words can stand alone?
    a. gastr
    b. carcin
    c. lapar
    d. pyr(e)
    _____

11. Which of the following Greek roots means vessel?
    a. angi
    b. bracy
    c. aden
    d. chir
    _____

12. Which of the following Greek roots means to increase?
    a. ede
    b. cau
    c. aux
    d. gno
    _____

13. An esthetician wishing to use the Greek root for ligaments should choose:
    a. ancon
    b. desm
    c. mel
    d. por
    _____

14. A word that suggests motion must have which of the following Greek root words?
    a. ba
    b. mit
    c. kine
    d. lal
    _____

15. Something that is hardened would have the Greek root word:
    a. thorac
    b. anthrop
    c. hygr
    d. scler
    _____

16. What does the Latin root word *gemin* mean?
    a. paired
    b. smooth
    c. light
    d. round
    _____

17. Which of the following Latin root words means to drag?
    a. ambul
    b. tuber
    c. fiss
    d. tract
    _____

18. Prefixes modify words by _____ them.
    a. quantifying
    b. qualifying
    c. both a and b
    d. neither a nor b
    _____

19. The meaning of the Greek prefix *cata-* means which of the following?
    a. outward or inside
    b. down or against
    c. with or together
    d. around or nearby
    _____

20. Which of the following Latin prefixes means beyond?
    a. ultra-
    b. red-
    c. contr-
    d. suf-
    _____

21. The most important clue a suffix provides is a word's:
    - a. spelling
    - b. language of origin
    - c. length
    - d. part of speech

    _____

22. When appended to a word, all of the following create nouns EXCEPT:
    - a. -itis
    - b. -oma
    - c. -icle
    - d. -gen

    _____

23. Of the following Greek suffixes, which means pertaining to or like?
    - a. -ida
    - b. -tic
    - c. -ode
    - d. -us

    _____

24. The Latin suffix _____ means inclination toward.
    - a. -acious
    - b. -esce
    - c. -ment
    - d. -trum

    _____

25. The correct pronunciation of the word *gnathitis* is:
    - a. guh-NAH-thus
    - b. gun-nuh-THAY-tuss
    - c. guh-NUH-thigh-tus
    - d. na-THIGH-tus

    _____

1. Which of the following procedures facilitates the elimination of small blood vessels, enlarged veins, and dilated capillaries?
   a. injectable filler
   b. medical peel
   c. Botox®
   d. sclerotherapy
   ____

2. Which of the following procedures belongs on the medical side of esthetics?
   a. microdermabrasion
   b. facial toning
   c. injection vein therapy
   d. all answers
   ____

3. Which of the following issues with dermal filler can the esthetician address with the client without consequence?
   a. best indications
   b. postcare procedures
   c. product durability
   d. all answers
   ____

4. All of the following impact the durability of dermal filler EXCEPT:
   a. product cost
   b. placement location
   c. placement depth
   d. session number
   ____

5. Which of the following describes the process of dermal filler?
   a. inexpensive
   b. time consuming
   c. comfortable
   d. none of these
   ____

6. The more deeply a product is placed, the more _____ it will absorb.
   a. weakly
   b. strongly
   c. quickly
   d. slowly
   ____

7. For how long will dermal filler reside in tissue?
   a. three weeks
   b. two months
   c. six months
   d. one year
   ____

8. In general, the effects of a Botox® treatment can be expected to last for how long?
   a. six to twelve months
   b. three to five months
   c. four to six weeks
   d. one to two weeks
   ____

9. To avoid bruising, how long before Botox® treatments should clients discontinue the use of aspirin and like products?
   a. two days
   b. five days
   c. one week
   d. two weeks
   ____

10. Dynamic movement of the neck and jaw result in what are known as _____ bands.
    a. corrective
    b. platsymal
    c. cleaving
    d. impulsive   _____

11. When the brow is evaluated for Botox® cosmetic treatment, all of the following should be considered EXCEPT:
    a. line depth
    b. glabellar involvement
    c. eyebrow color
    d. brow heaviness   _____

12. Which of the following types of line are often associated with skin laxity in the upper face?
    a. forehead
    b. crow's feet
    c. vertical lip
    d. marionette   _____

13. All of the following are natural dermal fillers EXCEPT:
    a. liquid silicone
    b. hyaluronic acid
    c. bovine collagen
    d. autologous collagen   _____

14. The wait time for bovine collagen allergy analysis is how long?
    a. 12 days
    b. 29 days
    c. 6 weeks
    d. 12 weeks   _____

15. A client with which of the following is NOT suited to bovine collagen treatment?
    a. lip augmentation
    b. crow's feet
    c. lactation
    d. acne scarring   _____

16. Unlike bovine collagen, human collagen has the benefit of:
    a. causing fewer allergic reactions
    b. shortening allergy testing
    c. having shorter durability
    d. requiring no skin testing   _____

17. Cosmoplast is used to treat which of the following?
    a. coarse rhytides around the mouth
    b. folds in the nasolabial area
    c. deep rhytides in the glabellar region
    d. all answers   _____

18. About what percent of hyaluronic acid is found in the skin?
    a. 15%
    b. 30%
    c. 50%
    d. 90%   _____

19. Which of the following hyaluronic acid products contains zinc, selenium, and embryonic extracts?
   a. Achal
   b. Hyacell
   c. Dermalive
   d. Dermadeep
   _____

20. All of the following hylans require U.S. Food and Drug Administration (FDA) approval EXCEPT:
   a. Matridur
   b. Hylaform
   c. Viscontour
   d. a and b
   _____

21. Crow's feet are often treated most effectively with which of the following?
   a. Botox® and dermal filler
   b. Botox® alone
   c. Botox® and glabella
   d. glabella and dermal filler
   _____

22. Studies have shown that women are about twice as likely to develop varicose veins because they:
   a. have twice as many veins
   b. cross their legs frequently
   c. drink about twice as much water
   d. have more muscles in the leg
   _____

23. Which of the following treatments injects a chemical irritant into a vein to eliminate lumen and improve vein appearance?
   a. cleaving
   b. dysphagia
   c. keratitis
   d. sclerotherapy
   _____

24. Which of the following is a characteristic of the chemical peels used by physicians?
   a. less chance of flaky skin
   b. reduced redness and edema
   c. heightened risk of scarring
   d. less intense action
   _____

25. When trichloroacetic acid (TCA) is applied to the skin, it acts as a cautery by doing which of the following?
   a. coagulating protein and causing frosting
   b. penetrating the papillary dermis
   c. flattening areas of scarring
   d. reducing instances of rhytides
   _____

CHAPTER 27—PLASTIC SURGERY PROCEDURES

1. Patients who are under local anesthesia with IV sedation are:
   a. susceptible to occasional discomfort
   b. asleep throughout their procedures
   c. unaware of any discomfort
   d. all answers ____

2. The medical term *rhytidectomy* derives in part from the Latin word *rhytid*, which means:
   a. face   c. lift
   b. remove   d. wrinkle ____

3. A rhytidectomy lifts least dramatically in which part of the face?
   a. lower   c. sides
   b. upper   d. all answers ____

4. Resurfacing best treats all of the following EXCEPT:
   a. superficial lines   c. deep sagging
   b. pigmentation issues d. skin irregularities ____

5. The typical face-lift client is about what age?
   a. 40–60   c. 20–30
   b. 30–40   d. 80 and older ____

6. The rhytidectomy procedure does which of the following?
   a. redistributes excess fat   c. hides excess skin
   b. tightens underlying muscles d. all answers ____

7. Smoking cessation is mandatory for at least one to two weeks before rhytidectomy because smoking:
   a. inhibits blood flow
   b. coats the skin with chemicals
   c. overstimulates the follicles
   d. none of these ____

8. In a rhytidectomy, which of the following planes involves only a skin flap?
   a. deep   c. medium
   b. combination   d. classic ____

9. Relative to a traditional face-lift, a thread lift is:
   a. more invasive to the skin
   b. less effective for the neck
   c. more complex technologically
   d. all answers ____

10. Both the classic and endoscopic forehead-lifts have a similar approach in which of the following?
    a. incision size
    b. incision placement
    c. muscle manipulation
    d. all answers
    _____

11. The best candidates for cosmetic blepharoplasty have which of the following?
    a. baggy lower eyelids
    b. dark circles under the eyes
    c. sagging eyebrows
    d. fine lines around the eyes
    _____

12. Blepharoplasty may be performed in which of the following?
    a. hospital
    b. surgeon's office
    c. outpatient facility
    d. all answers
    _____

13. When the chin is weak or receding, which of the following occurs?
    a. nose looks larger
    b. neck looks less fatty
    c. forehead appears smaller
    d. all answers
    _____

14. An implant to improve the shape of the chin is known as:
    a. blepharoplasty
    b. mentoplasty
    c. mastopexy
    d. rhytidectomy
    _____

15. Breast implants impact which of the following?
    a. fertility
    b. nursing ability
    c. pregnancy
    d. none of these
    _____

16. Breasts with ptosis are which of the following?
    a. lumpy
    b. perky
    c. droopy
    d. full
    _____

17. Women with breasts of which size have the longest-lasting effects of mastopexy?
    a. large
    b. medium
    c. small
    d. all answers
    _____

18. Mastopexy generally takes about how many hours?
    a. 1 1/2–3 1/2
    b. 3 1/2–5 1/2
    c. 5 1/2–7 1/2
    d. 7 1/2–8 1/2
    _____

19. Breast reduction surgery removes which of the following?
    a. skin only
    b. skin and fatty tissue
    c. both a and b
    d. neither a nor b

    ____

20. About _____ of breast cancer patients opt to have breast reconstructive work.
    a. 95%
    b. 75%
    c. 55%
    d. 35%

    ____

21. Which of the following breast reconstruction procedures keeps tissue attached to its original site via its blood supply?
    a. distant or flap reconstruction
    b. skin expansion
    c. free flap
    d. musculocutaneous flap

    ____

22. The procedure that smoothes, firms, and flattens the abdomen and thins the waist is known as:
    a. abdominoplasty
    b. mastectomy
    c. endoscopy
    d. mentoplasty

    ____

23. Which of the following surgical procedures is conducted for morbid obesity?
    a. abdominal
    b. circumareolar
    c. bariatric
    d. liposuction

    ____

24. Candidates for abdominoplasty should avoid which of the following before the procedure?
    a. sun exposure
    b. smoking
    c. radical diet
    d. all answers

    ____

25. Which of the following is considered a body contouring procedure?
    a. rhytidectomy
    b. mastopexy
    c. rhinoplasty
    d. blepharoplasty

    ____

CHAPTER 28—THE ESTHETICIAN'S ROLE IN PRE- AND POST-MEDICAL TREATMENTS

1. Which of the following are ablative laser procedures?
    a. peeling
    b. resurfacing
    c. fractional resurfacing
    d. all answers
    ____

2. An ablative procedure does which of the following?
    a. disrupts the epidermis
    b. smoothes the skin's surface
    c. removes excess fatty tissue
    d. sloughs off dead skin cells
    ____

3. In preparation for surgery or an ablative procedure, which of the following can help stimulate circulation, remove wastes, and minimize swelling?
    a. microdermabrasion
    b. enzyme peel
    c. lymphatic drainage
    d. ultrasonic
    ____

4. Superficial chemical peels like AHA, BHA, and retinoic acid are all designed to:
    a. darken the skin
    b. exfoliate the epidermis
    c. highlight areas of pigmentation
    d. all answers
    ____

5. Which of the following enzymes is most gentle?
    a. pectinase
    b. bromelain
    c. trypsine
    d. papain
    ____

6. In ultrasonic, which of the following occurs during the cavitation step?
    a. skin peeling
    b. serum penetration
    c. skin lightening
    d. tissue removal
    ____

7. Which of the following procedures has muscle-strengthening aspects?
    a. lymphatic drainage
    b. enzyme peel
    c. contact dermatitis
    d. microcurrent facial toning
    ____

8. For maximal impact, lymphatic drainage should be conducted how far in advance of a procedure?
    a. five days
    b. seven days
    c. two weeks
    d. four weeks
    ____

9. As part of presurgical home care, the skin-care kit is generally started how long before any procedure?
    a. four weeks
    b. eight weeks
    c. three months
    d. six months
    _____

10. In general, which of the following components is unique to prelaser home care?
    a. hydroquinone
    b. AHA
    c. sunscreen
    d. moisturizer
    _____

11. Which of the following is commonly recommended as a hydrator/moisturizer for home use prior to surgery?
    a. vitamin A
    b. chamomile
    c. amino acid
    d. bioflavinoid
    _____

12. All of the following are applied in the morning as part of prelaser home care EXCEPT:
    a. retinoic acid
    b. cleanser
    c. moisturizer
    d. lightener
    _____

13. All of the following are eye creams used in presurgery home care EXCEPT:
    a. arnica
    b. sodium hyaluronate
    c. allantoin
    d. vitamin E
    _____

14. Which of the following occurs 5–10 days after CO_2/erbium:YAG laser resurfacing?
    a. the client incorporates mineral makeup as camouflage
    b. the client applies solution soaks every 2–3 hours
    c. a light AHA exfoliation is performed on the client
    d. ice packs are applied to reduce swelling and discomfort
    _____

15. In face-lift post-operative care, manual lymphatic drainage is applied how long after the procedure?
    a. three weeks
    b. two weeks
    c. eight to fifteen days
    d. seven days
    _____

16. In days 8–15 following a face-lift, the client should adopt a cleansing routine that starts with which of the following?
    a. moisturizer
    b. antibiotic
    c. hydrogen peroxide
    d. none of these
    _____

17. At which point in face-lift post-operative care is a facial bra used?
    a. three weeks
    b. two weeks
    c. eight to fifteen days
    d. one week
    _____

18. Of the following procedures, which has the shortest recovery time?
    a. laser resurfacing
    b. eye-lift
    c. face-lift
    d. chin liposuction   ____

19. At what point in eye-lift post-operative care does the nurse or doctor remove the client's sutures?
    a. days one to seven
    b. days five to ten
    c. days seven to twelve
    d. two to three weeks   ____

20. For the client, the most critical time for infection is the _____ after surgery.
    a. second week
    b. next month
    c. first days
    d. next year   ____

Part 7: Business Skills

CHAPTER 29—FINANCIAL BUSINESS SKILLS

1. In business, a plan of action is called a:
   a. company blueprint
   b. business plan
   c. balance sheet
   d. capital venture _____

2. Which of the following sections of a business plan contains such items as key personnel and their roles and policies and procedures for staff?
   a. marketing strategy
   b. executive summary
   c. strategic design
   d. operations _____

3. All of the following are sections of a conventional business plan EXCEPT:
   a. personal participation
   b. strategic design
   c. financial information
   d. marketing strategy _____

4. The entity known as the four P's belongs in which section of a business plan?
   a. executive summary
   b. marketing strategy
   c. strategic design
   d. operations _____

5. An analysis of a business's strengths, weaknesses, opportunities, and threats (SWOT) belongs in which section of a business plan?
   a. strategic design and development
   b. financial information
   c. marketing strategy
   d. executive summary _____

6. For which of the following sections of a business plan is the audience particularly important?
   a. marketing strategy
   b. financial information
   c. operations
   d. executive summary _____

7. The true "nuts and bolts" of a business are reflection in which section of a business plan?
   a. executive summary
   b. financial summary
   c. operations
   d. strategic design _____

8. All of the following are sources for raising capital EXCEPT:
   a. stocks
   b. investors
   c. savings
   d. loans _____

9. A credit score helps determine which of the following?
   a. success of a product in the market
   b. number of venture capitalists
   c. size of a business's budget
   d. ability to secure loans   _____

10. An outside vendor or private individual who contributes money to a business is known as a:
   a. contributing partner   c. venture capitalist
   b. equity owner   d. promissory holder   _____

11. Which of the following professional resources provides free online and face-to-face business counseling, mentoring, and training?
   a. Small Business Development Centers
   b. Service Core of Retired Executives
   c. Small Business Administration
   d. Small Business Training Network   _____

12. The standard procedures established by the accounting profession to govern such documents as the balance sheet and income statement are called the:
   a. Generally Accepted Accounting Principles
   b. Liabilities of Owner's Equity
   c. Small Business Training Requirements
   d. all answers   _____

13. Which of the following documents provides a long-term view of a business's financial picture?
   a. balance sheet
   b. cash flow statement
   c. profit-and-loss statement
   d. none of these answers   _____

14. All of the following are assets for an esthetics business EXCEPT:
   a. skin-care products   c. equipment loan
   b. facility itself   d. computer equipment   _____

15. The total amount of money a business takes in from selling products and service is called:
   a. break-even point   c. equity limit
   b. gross profit   d. balance point   _____

16. Businesses that safeguard themselves against loss or damage are said to exercise what is called:
   a. owner equity   c. risk management
   b. liability insurance   d. all answers   _____

17. Estheticians who meet the lawful IRS definition of "independent contractor" are responsible for paying which of the following?
    a. self-employment tax
    b. income tax
    c. periodic estimated taxes
    d. all answers
    _____

18. An Individual Taxpayer Identification Number (ITIN) is assigned to which of the following parties?
    a. U.S. resident alien
    b. small business owner
    c. independent contractor
    d. all answers
    _____

19. Which of the following forms summarizes an employee's wages for a specified calendar year?
    a. I-9
    b. W-2
    c. W-4
    d. 1099
    _____

20. Employers use which of the following forms to report federal estimated tax payments?
    a. 941
    b. 940
    c. 1040-ES
    d. 1-ES
    _____

CHAPTER 30—MARKETING

1. The four P's are factors generally referred to as the:
   a. marketing mix
   b. demographic breakdown
   c. promotional mix
   d. marketing plan _____

2. Which of the four P's accounts for the distribution channel or method for delivering goods and services to clients?
   a. product
   b. promotion
   c. place
   d. price _____

3. Which of the following is an example of indirect cost of providing esthetics services?
   a. technician's salary
   b. rent on the facility
   c. enzymes for peels
   d. all answers _____

4. In the marketing mix, which of the following is an example of a "place"?
   a. wholesaler
   b. manufacturer
   c. distributor
   d. all answers _____

5. All of the following are part of the promotion mix EXCEPT:
   a. personal selling
   b. sales promotion
   c. customer relations
   d. public relations _____

6. In the "who, what, where, and how" of marketing communications, the "what" refers to the:
   a. message being conveyed
   b. budget for marketing
   c. product being marketed
   d. value desired for the client _____

7. Which mode of advertising is an inexpensive way to promote products and services?
   a. magazines
   b. classified ads
   c. newspapers
   d. radio and television _____

8. The mode of advertising that tends to be least expensive is:
   a. classified ads
   b. newspapers
   c. direct mail
   d. radio and television _____

9. As public relations tools, advertorials, press releases, and media kits are designed to target:
   a. magazine editors
   b. print journalists
   c. broadcast journalists
   d. all answers _____

10. A salon that wishes to boost its image in the public should do which of the following?
    a. redesign dated product displays
    b. offer nonallergenic products
    c. offer free facials for battered women
    d. all answers ____

11. One significant challenge of direct marketing is:
    a. distributing direct mail pieces
    b. prompting recipients to respond
    c. earning slots on "do not call" lists
    d. all answers ____

12. Which of the following statements about personal selling is true?
    a. the most effective personal sellers are excellent communicators
    b. it is less cost-effective than other approaches
    c. it should be done by top staff only
    d. none of these ____

13. To ensure the success of personal selling, salon owners should do which of the following first?
    a. hire new staff   c. rearrange the salon
    b. add new products   d. provide staff training ____

14. The goal of a sales promotion is to:
    a. train staff   c. boost business
    b. educate clients   d. all answers ____

15. A detailed plan that defines a business's target market and states its unique selling proposition is called a(n) _____ plan.
    a. business   c. standout
    b. marketing   d. announcement ____

16. When marketing skin care, all of the following are primary objectives to consider EXCEPT:
    a. promote old products with new
    b. fill in slow periods
    c. increase retail sales
    d. encourage repeat business ____

17. The highlight of a salon's brochure or menu of services should be:
    a. policies   c. services
    b. graphics   d. staff ____

18. What is the primary goal of any website?
    a. showcase a business's products
    b. create an attractive image
    c. sell a business's services
    d. entice visitors to call or visit   ____

19. To evaluate how well it is doing, a salon can do which of the following?
    a. analyze the overall performance of individual products
    b. study individual client profiles
    c. look at individual employee performance in depth
    d. all answers   ____

20. Which of the following type of card is an inappropriate use for the salon's computer technology?
    a. referral   c. birthday
    b. business   d. thank-you   ____

Part I: Orientation

CHAPTER 1—CHANGES IN ESTHETIC OPPORTUNITIES

1. C	6. A	11. B	16. D
2. A	7. D	12. D	17. A
3. D	8. B	13. C	18. B
4. B	9. C	14. B	19. C
5. C	10. A	15. A	20. D

Part II: General Sciences

CHAPTER 2—INFECTION CONTROL

1. A	14. D	27. B	40. A	53. A
2. B	15. A	28. D	41. D	54. B
3. C	16. B	29. C	42. C	55. A
4. B	17. C	30. A	43. B	56. D
5. A	18. D	31. B	44. C	57. C
6. D	19. A	32. C	45. A	58. B
7. C	20. B	33. D	46. D	59. A
8. B	21. A	34. B	47. C	60. B
9. A	22. C	35. A	48. B	61. D
10. C	23. D	36. A	49. A	62. C
11. D	24. B	37. C	50. D	63. A
12. B	25. A	38. B	51. C	64. B
13. A	26. C	39. D	52. D	65. C

CHAPTER 3—ADVANCED HISTOLOGY OF THE CELL AND SKIN BY PETER T. PUGLIESE, M.D.

1. D	12. D	23. B	34. D	45. A
2. A	13. A	24. D	35. B	46. C
3. C	14. C	25. A	36. A	47. D
4. B	15. B	26. C	37. C	48. B
5. A	16. D	27. B	38. D	49. C
6. C	17. A	28. A	39. B	50. A
7. D	18. B	29. D	40. A	51. B
8. B	19. C	30. C	41. B	52. D
9. A	20. D	31. B	42. C	53. C
10. B	21. C	32. A	43. D	54. B
11. A	22. A	33. C	44. B	55. A

CHAPTER 4—HORMONES

1. B	6. D	11. C	16. B	21. C
2. D	7. C	12. B	17. A	22. B
3. C	8. D	13. D	18. C	23. A
4. B	9. B	14. A	19. B	24. D
5. A	10. A	15. D	20. D	25. B

CHAPTER 5—ANATOMY AND PHYSIOLOGY: MUSCLES AND NERVES

1. A	11. C	21. C
2. C	12. D	22. D
3. B	13. A	23. B
4. D	14. B	24. A
5. A	15. C	25. B
6. B	16. A	26. D
7. C	17. D	27. C
8. D	18. B	28. A
9. B	19. C	29. B
10. B	20. A	30. C

CHAPTER 6—ANATOMY AND PHYSIOLOGY: THE CARDIOVASCULAR AND LYMPHATIC SYSTEMS

1. A	11. A
2. B	12. D
3. C	13. C
4. C	14. B
5. D	15. B
6. B	16. A
7. A	17. D
8. C	18. C
9. B	19. A
10. D	20. D

CHAPTER 7—CHEMISTRY AND BIOCHEMISTRY

1. C	11. C
2. C	12. D
3. D	13. A
4. A	14. B
5. B	15. A
6. A	16. D
7. C	17. C
8. B	18. B
9. D	19. A
10. A	20. D

CHAPTER 8—LASER, LIGHT ENERGY, AND RADIO-FREQUENCY THERAPY

1. A	8. C	15. B	22. C	29. C
2. C	9. C	16. A	23. A	30. B
3. B	10. A	17. A	24. D	31. D
4. D	11. B	18. D	25. A	32. B
5. A	12. D	19. B	26. B	33. A
6. B	13. C	20. D	27. C	
7. D	14. A	21. D	28. A	

Part III: Skin Sciences

CHAPTER 9—NUTRITION AND STRESS MANAGEMENT

1. D	11. C
2. C	12. B
3. B	13. D
4. D	14. A
5. A	15. D
6. B	16. B
7. C	17. C
8. D	18. A
9. A	19. D
10. C	20. B

CHAPTER 10—ADVANCED SKIN DISORDERS: SKIN IN DISTRESS

1. C	11. B	21. D	31. A
2. A	12. C	22. C	32. B
3. D	13. B	23. A	33. B
4. B	14. A	24. D	34. C
5. B	15. B	25. B	35. D
6. A	16. D	26. A	36. A
7. C	17. C	27. B	37. B
8. D	18. B	28. D	38. D
9. A	19. A	29. C	39. C
10. D	20. B	30. C	40. D

CHAPTER 11—SKIN TYPING AND AGING ANALYSIS

1. A	6. D	11. A	16. A
2. D	7. C	12. B	17. C
3. B	8. B	13. C	18. D
4. B	9. D	14. D	19. B
5. C	10. D	15. B	20. A

CHAPTER 12—SKIN CARE PRODUCTS: INGREDIENTS AND CHEMISTRY

1. B	13. A	25. D	37. C	49. A
2. C	14. B	26. A	38. B	50. C
3. A	15. B	27. C	39. A	51. D
4. D	16. D	28. B	40. C	52. B
5. B	17. C	29. A	41. D	53. C
6. A	18. A	30. B	42. B	54. B
7. C	19. B	31. D	43. A	55. C
8. D	20. D	32. C	44. C	56. D
9. A	21. A	33. A	45. C	57. A
10. B	22. C	34. B	46. D	58. A
11. D	23. B	35. D	47. A	59. B
12. C	24. D	36. D	48. B	60. C

CHAPTER 13—BOTANICALS AND AROMATHERAPY

1. D	11. A	21. C
2. C	12. C	22. C
3. A	13. D	23. D
4. B	14. A	24. A
5. D	15. B	25. C
6. A	16. B	26. D
7. B	17. C	27. B
8. C	18. D	28. A
9. D	19. A	29. C
10. B	20. B	30. D

CHAPTER 14—INGREDIENTS AND PRODUCTS FOR SKIN ISSUES

1. A	8. B	15. A	22. D	29. A
2. B	9. D	16. B	23. A	30. D
3. D	10. A	17. C	24. B	31. C
4. A	11. C	18. D	25. C	32. B
5. D	12. B	19. B	26. D	33. D
6. C	13. D	20. C	27. C	34. B
7. D	14. C	21. A	28. B	35. A

CHAPTER 15—PHARMACOLOGY FOR ESTHETICIANS

1. B	11. A	21. A	31. D
2. A	12. D	22. B	32. A
3. C	13. B	23. B	33. C
4. D	14. C	24. C	34. B
5. B	15. A	25. D	35. D
6. C	16. D	26. C	36. C
7. A	17. A	27. A	37. A
8. D	18. D	28. B	38. B
9. C	19. C	29. C	39. D
10. B	20. D	30. B	40. C

Part IV: Esthetics

CHAPTER 16—ADVANCED FACIAL TECHNIQUES

1. B	11. B	21. C	31. B	41. A
2. D	12. D	22. A	32. D	42. D
3. A	13. C	23. B	33. A	43. D
4. C	14. D	24. D	34. D	44. B
5. A	15. A	25. C	35. B	45. B
6. B	16. D	26. B	36. C	46. C
7. D	17. B	27. D	37. A	47. A
8. D	18. C	28. A	38. B	48. D
9. C	19. A	29. C	39. C	49. B
10. A	20. D	30. C	40. D	50. C

CHAPTER 17—ADVANCED SKIN CARE MASSAGE

1. D	11. B	21. C
2. A	12. C	22. D
3. C	13. D	23. C
4. A	14. B	24. B
5. D	15. A	25. A
6. B	16. A	26. D
7. B	17. C	27. C
8. C	18. D	28. B
9. D	19. B	29. A
10. A	20. A	30. D

CHAPTER 18—ADVANCED FACIAL DEVICES

1. A	11. B	21. B	31. A
2. B	12. D	22. D	32. B
3. D	13. A	23. B	33. C
4. C	14. B	24. C	34. B
5. A	15. D	25. A	35. D
6. B	16. C	26. A	36. A
7. A	17. C	27. D	37. D
8. D	18. A	28. B	38. B
9. C	19. A	29. C	39. C
10. A	20. C	30. D	40. A

CHAPTER 19—HAIR REMOVAL

1. C	7. A	13. B	19. B	25. D
2. A	8. A	14. C	20. A	26. C
3. D	9. B	15. C	21. D	27. A
4. D	10. A	16. D	22. C	28. C
5. A	11. B	17. A	23. A	29. B
6. D	12. C	18. C	24. B	30. D

31. C	36. D	41. A	46. D	51. C
32. A	37. B	42. B	47. B	52. B
33. B	38. A	43. A	48. C	53. A
34. C	39. D	44. D	49. A	54. B
35. D	40. C	45. C	50. D	55. C

CHAPTER 20—ADVANCED MAKEUP

1. C	16. A	31. B
2. D	17. D	32. C
3. A	18. B	33. A
4. C	19. C	34. D
5. B	20. C	35. B
6. D	21. A	36. C
7. A	22. D	37. D
8. D	23. B	38. A
9. C	24. A	39. B
10. B	25. D	40. C
11. A	26. C	41. D
12. D	27. B	42. A
13. C	28. C	43. C
14. B	29. A	44. B
15. A	30. D	45. D

Part V: Spas

CHAPTER 21—SPA TREATMENTS

1. B	11. B	21. D	31. D
2. D	12. D	22. A	32. C
3. A	13. A	23. C	33. D
4. C	14. C	24. B	34. B
5. B	15. B	25. D	35. A
6. D	16. D	26. C	36. D
7. C	17. A	27. B	37. C
8. A	18. B	28. C	38. B
9. B	19. C	29. B	39. A
10. C	20. B	30. A	40. D

CHAPTER 22—ALTERNATIVE THERAPIES

1. D	5. A	9. A
2. A	6. C	10. B
3. C	7. D	11. C
4. B	8. B	12. D

13. C	19. B	25. D
14. A	20. A	26. C
15. A	21. D	27. A
16. D	22. C	28. B
17. A	23. B	29. D
18. C	24. A	

CHAPTER 23—AYURVEDA THEORY AND TREATMENTS

1. A	11. C	21. A	31. B
2. D	12. D	22. D	32. A
3. B	13. A	23. B	33. C
4. C	14. A	24. D	34. B
5. D	15. C	25. D	35. D
6. D	16. D	26. C	36. A
7. A	17. C	27. B	37. B
8. B	18. C	28. A	38. C
9. B	19. B	29. C	39. D
10. C	20. A	30. D	40. C

Part VI: Medical

CHAPTER 24—WORKING IN A MEDICAL SETTING

1. B	6. A	11. A	16. A
2. C	7. A	12. B	17. D
3. D	8. B	13. D	18. C
4. D	9. D	14. C	19. B
5. C	10. C	15. B	20. A

CHAPTER 25—MEDICAL TERMINOLOGY

1. A	6. D	11. A	16. A	21. D
2. C	7. A	12. C	17. D	22. C
3. B	8. C	13. B	18. C	23. B
4. B	9. B	14. C	19. B	24. A
5. D	10. D	15. D	20. A	25. D

CHAPTER 26—MEDICAL INTERVENTION

1. D	6. C	11. C	16. D	21. A
2. C	7. D	12. D	17. A	22. B
3. D	8. B	13. A	18. C	23. D
4. A	9. A	14. B	19. B	24. C
5. B	10. B	15. C	20. B	25. A

CHAPTER 27—PLASTIC SURGERY PROCEDURES

1. A	6. B	11. A	16. C	21. D
2. D	7. A	12. D	17. C	22. A
3. B	8. D	13. A	18. A	23. C
4. C	9. B	14. B	19. C	24. D
5. A	10. C	15. D	20. B	25. B

CHAPTER 28—THE ESTHETICIAN'S ROLE IN PRE- AND POST-MEDICAL TREATMENTS

1. D	6. A	11. D	16. C
2. A	7. D	12. A	17. D
3. C	8. C	13. C	18. B
4. B	9. B	14. B	19. B
5. D	10. A	15. A	20. C

Part VII: Business Skills

CHAPTER 29—FINANCIAL BUSINESS SKILLS

1. B	6. B	11. B	16. C
2. D	7. D	12. A	17. D
3. A	8. A	13. C	18. A
4. C	9. D	14. C	19. B
5. A	10. C	15. B	20. C

CHAPTER 30—MARKETING

1. A	6. A	11. B	16. A
2. C	7. B	12. A	17. C
3. B	8. A	13. D	18. D
4. D	9. D	14. C	19. D
5. C	10. C	15. B	20. B